The Structural Basis of Behavior

J. A. DEUTSCH

The Structural Basis
of
Behavior

THE UNIVERSITY OF CHICAGO PRESS

LIBRARY OF CONGRESS CATALOG NUMBER: 60-12466

THE UNIVERSITY OF CHICAGO PRESS, CHICAGO 37
CAMBRIDGE UNIVERSITY PRESS, LONDON, N.W. I, ENGLAND
THE UNIVERSITY OF TORONTO PRESS, TORONTO 5, CANADA

© 1960 BY THE UNIVERSITY OF CHICAGO. PUBLISHED 1960
SECOND IMPRESSION 1964. COMPOSED AND PRINTED BY THE
UNIVERSITY OF CHICAGO PRESS, CHICAGO, ILLINOIS, U.S.A.

To Diana

Preface

This book presents a set of theories. These theories are structural models or explanations of behavior in terms of postulated mechanisms, such as might be found in the nervous system of animals or such as might be built as machines to manifest the same behavior as animals. The book accordingly covers the salient experimental, both physiological and psychological, evidence in such fields as motivation, learning, extinction, reasoning, and shape recognition and shows how this evidence can be deduced from the proposed theoretical systems. Further deductions from these theoretical systems have been made and an account is given of fresh experimental tests of these predictions. The success of these theories in predicting experimental outcomes has been such that perhaps some excuse will be found for the connected and developed statement of the theoretical framework as it appears in this book.

I wish to thank the Medical Research Council, without whose support much of this work would not have been done. I am indebted to many friends at the Institute of Experimental Psychology, Oxford, for their interest and especially to A. J. Watson, J. von Wright, and K. Danziger for many valuable discussions. I also wish to express my gratitude for the advice of Dr. H. Kay. I am also grateful to Professor Humphrey and Professor Oldfield for sympathy and encouragement while working in their laboratory. I am indebted to H. Solomon for his careful reading of the manuscript to which was due the ironing-out of many obscurities.

My thanks are due to the editor and publisher of the *Quarterly Journal of Experimental Psychology* for permission to reproduce the major portion of the article entitled "A Machine with Insight" (pp. 7–11), which appeared in **6**, 6–11 of this journal in February, 1954, and to copy Figures 1, 2, 4, and 5, which were also a part of this article. This now forms part of chapter x. I should also like to thank them for permission to reproduce a figure (Fig. I) from an article by

J. A. Deutsch and W. S. Anthony (*Quarterly Journal of Experimental Psychology*, **10** [February, 1958], 23). The article is entitled "Blocking the Incorrect Alley in a Two-Drive Learning Situation."

I am also indebted to the editor and publishers of the *Psychological Review* for allowing me to reproduce in chapter viii the article entitled "The Inadequacy of the Hullian Derivations of Reasoning and Latent Learning" and the figures contained therein, which appeared in the *Psychological Review*, **63** (1956), 389–99.

Lastly I should like to thank the editor and publishers of the *British Journal of Psychology* for permission to reproduce in part, with some alteration, a paper entitled "A Theory of Shape Recognition" (*British Journal of Psychology*, **46** [1955], 30–37) to form the first part of chapter xi. They have also kindly permitted me to draw upon a paper entitled "A Theory of Insight, Reasoning and Latent Learning" (*British Journal of Psychology*, **47** [1956], 117–25). This has been almost completely recast in chapter ix, where the figures used are similar to those appearing in the above-mentioned article.

Contents

I

Explanation and Its Classification

In what follows an attempt is made to explain some of the experimental evidence amassed by psychologists. This evidence has been collected by the use of methods whose sophistication leaves little to be desired and whose ingenuity stands favorable comparison with that displayed in other sciences. Remarkable techniques have been developed for the purpose of collecting data about the behavior of animal organisms under rigorously controlled conditions and for assessing these by elaborate statistical procedure. In this way a large mass of scientifically impeccable evidence has been built up and the pile is daily augmented. We cannot call it an edifice, for in spite of the general agreement about the method of making the bricks, there is no accepted way of putting them together. There is no concord among psychologists about what the facts they have accumulated are evidence for. This does not mean that they are merely in disagreement about the edifice they wish to erect; they have not decided even what constitutes a building. That is, not only do they disagree about the explanation of their findings, but they are not clear about what it would be to explain them. As a result it is not sufficient only to put forward a theory to explain the facts; it is also necessary to put forward a theory to justify the type of theory put forward. This is the reason for beginning with a discussion on explanation. There is little agreement on this topic and no general consensus of opinion on the various issues involved, which is not very surprising, as no one has been clear about what the issues are.

   It will here be argued that explanations can be divided into two main classes. The first is of the descriptive or generalizatory type. The second is of the structural, neurophysiological, or mechanical type. It will further be argued that there are two stages in a structural or neurophysiological explanation. The first stage is the devis-

[1]

ing of a system whose properties tally with our observations of behavior. The second is the identification of the elements of this system in neural terms. It is argued that a psychological theorist need only be concerned with the first stage.

i

THE GENERALIZATORY TYPE
OF EXPLANATION

Suppose we are watching a rat running through a maze for a food reward. It runs straight to the goal without entering a blind alley. One of the ways of explaining such a performance is to show that the behavior of this particular rat is but an instance of the behavior of animals in learning situations. We can thus demonstrate that the particular behavior we see is deducible from a general statement or a set of general statements. These general statements are supplemented by propositions equating, let us say, the maze with another learning situation and from these two the rat's learning in the maze can be deduced.

It should be clear that the kind of explanation adopted is basically that a particular instance is subsumed under a statement summarizing a number of similar phenomena or shown to be an instance of a general case. The statement to be explained is shown to be an instance or special case of a number of generally observed phenomena in combination. In no sense can the particular observation be said to be a product of the generally observed phenomena. A rat's learning is not caused or produced by other rats learning, it is only another instance of this fact. Nor is a rat's learning caused or produced through a chain of cause and effect from the principles of conditioning; it is only deducible from them. It is deducible as a special instance of their operation, a consequence which is only logical.

Therefore when we adopt this type of explanation we should not be under the illusion that we have found a mechanism or a cause of behavior. To do this is to induce a type of thinking characteristic of medieval schoolmen. A poppy was said to make one drowsy because of its *vis dormitiva* or soporific power. A causal efficacy was attributed to a class property. It is easy enough to see this error in a simple case but it becomes more insidious when the logical interrelationship linking two statements becomes more complex.

This applies especially when we come to two developments of the

[2]

generalizatory method of explanation. The first development occurs where we observe that two events are regularly associated. For instance a stimulus may be regularly associated with a response. However, the second member may on occasion be present without the first's being observable; a response may occur without any apparent stimulus. In this case we are at liberty to extrapolate from the observed correlation between stimuli and responses by assuming stimuli to be present even though they are in fact inaccessible to observation. Having done this we can then attempt to derive these cases and their other properties from the usual premises about the observed conjunction between stimulus and response. It is in this way that Hull introduces his drive stimuli (S_D) and the fractional anticipatory goal stimulus (S_g). In these cases Hull infers from observed stimuli to unobserved stimuli, and is then enabled to apply the generalizations he has obtained concerning the observed conjunction more widely. Apart from the fact that the premises he uses have been applied to a case where there is less experimental warrant for doing so than when there is no such extrapolation, the derivation of a particular piece of behavior proceeds in the same way as hitherto. The behavior to be explained is treated as a particular instance of more general tendencies. However, the element of inference in this explanation makes it appear that we have in some way discovered or suggested a mechanism which produces the behavior under consideration. But all that we have done is to extend inductively the generalization or the group of generalizations of which the behavior to be explained is an instance.

The second development which appears on the surface to provide a causal explanation of behavior occurs in the so-called "intervening-variable" type of explanation. Here we begin with an observed correlation between phenomena. Supposing we have a box with a row of numbers on it, some blank panels, and a few colored buttons on the side. Now we find that if we press the buttons with numbers and then the red button, certain other numbers will appear on the blank panels. We repeat this process using buttons with other numbers and then the red button, and we find that the numbers on the blank panels always represent the sum of the other buttons we have pressed. If on the other hand we press the green buttons with the same numbers we obtain the multiple of the numbers indicated on the buttons appearing on the blank panel. We may then ask, "Why do we obtain different results when we press the green button and the

[3]

red button?" We can say that different processes intervene between the pressing of these buttons and the appearance of the numbers on the blank panels. The process which intervenes in one case is that of addition. The process which intervenes in the other is multiplication. We can then go on to say that multiplication or addition functions as an intervening variable. However, such a variable functions only descriptively, not causally. Multiplication does not cause a certain number to appear after the green button has been pressed; it is the interplay of the components of the machine that actually produces the result. We cannot hope to find any part in the machine which corresponds to multiplication by taking it to pieces. Multiplication is simply a name for what the machine does on certain occasions. In this way the use of the intervening variable "multiplication" is similar in this case to saying that the machine multiplies. This statement functions as an explanation only in the manner already discussed.

It is perhaps easier to see this in the example constructed above than in the psychological literature, because in the case of the machine we already know how it works. However, even such an eminent theorist as Tolman, for instance, considers that "retentivity" and "discriminatory capacity" are intervening variables and that they are part of the causal sequences between things like environmental stimuli and behavior (Tolman, *Collected Papers*, p. 119). (He also includes things like the laws of motivation, perception, and memory.)

Again, Hull, throughout the last chapter of his last book, speaks of general tendencies as mechanisms or devices. For instance, "To meet this type of emergency, evolution has developed a second automatic device. This is the primitive capacity to learn, to profit by past experience. Learning thus constitutes the *second major automatic adaptive behavior mechanism*" (p. 348). Another good example of this is to be found in Hull's *Essentials of Behavior* (p. 29): "Strictly speaking a habit is never observed as such, since it is hidden in the nervous system of the subject. We can observe the habit only indirectly by observing the molar (macroscopic) behavior of its possessor as it is mediated by previously formed habits. This means that habit ($_sH_R$) is a symbolic construct." Hull uses "symbolic construct" interchangeably with "intervening variable." In his paper on "the problem of intervening variables in molar behavior theory" he quotes various examples of intervening variables. He mentions

[4]

molecules, atoms, protons, electrons, and the like as examples from physics. Then he mentions anger (which he calls an unobserved intervening variable), perception, hypothesis, expectation, need, cognition, psychological force as examples from authors like Carnap, Brunswik, Tolman, and Buxton. His general criterion for regarding anything as an intervening variable seems to be that it is not directly observable. This criterion leads to the collocation of many unrelated entities. Things may not be directly observable for many different reasons. One may be that they are inaccessible to observation in such a way that better methods of observation would render them observable. Into this category fall such things as atoms and molecules. Another may be that there is really nothing to observe beyond what we can observe already. We should not be able to see hypotheses, perception, or psychological force, however good our microscopes.

One of the reasons for the confusion which has arisen may be that the general statements which function as premises in these theories express connections between events which can be regarded as causal. "The greater the need, the greater the speed of response." Therefore when we explain why a particular animal runs faster down an alley by pointing to the hours of food deprivation it has undergone, and quoting the general law, we are in a sense giving a causal explanation. However, we are still explaining a particular connection (causal or other) of two events by saying that they are each members of larger classes and that these two classes are regularly connected (causally or otherwise). But somehow the causal content of the premises is illicitly and tacitly transferred to the relation between the premises and their conclusions. The theory which is built up is then regarded as portraying the causal structure or the mechanism underlying the particular instances which it explains.

ii

STRUCTURAL EXPLANATION

There is of course nothing wrong with a theoretical system which explains a particular case by showing that it is merely a member of a more numerous set of instances. It is not intended in any way to disparage such a useful procedure. It is not dangerous in itself but only when it is confused with another radically different type of explanation. This is a structural type of explanation, where an event

lained by being deduced as the property of a structure, sys-
r mechanism, and not as an instance of events in its own class.
classical case which exemplifies this distinction is between
's law and the kinetic theory of gases. Whereas Boyle's law is a
ural statement about the observed causal connections between
temperature and pressure and the volume of a gas, the kinetic theory, though it can be said to explain the same particular instances as
Boyle's law, does so in a different manner. It explains the phenomena by postulating that gases have a certain structure. The
postulation of this structure of molecules forms a hypothesis from
which the observations concerning the volume of gases follow. The
hypothesis itself does not contain the observations to be explained,
and consequently the particular instances when explained by the
hypothesis are not merely shown to be another case of a similar set
of instances.

We may at this point return to the previously quoted example of
the adding and multiplying machine. We can explain any particular
arithmetical operation it makes by saying that it adds when a certain button is pressed or multiplies when another button is pressed.
This is the same kind of explanation as Boyle's law. On the other
hand we can ask why multiplication takes place at all. We can then
have recourse to a structural explanation. We can say that the machine is made up of various types of component and specify the interrelationships of such components. From this we are able to predict the calculations which the machine performs on all conceivable
occasions.

There are three types of classification of psychological theorizing
commonly employed, which partially overlap with the distinction
the writer wishes to draw. These are: (1) "the hypothetico-deduc-
tive method," (2) "the mathematical model," and (3) "hypothetical
construct." These will be dealt with in turn to show wherein they
are ambiguous and misleading.

It is first to be noted that in the structural type of explanation,
also, premises are set up and from these deductions are made when
we use the theory as an explanatory tool. Now one of the criteria of
scientific acceptability has been the use of the so-called hypothetico-
deductive method, which is said to be one of the special characteristics of one kind of psychological theory. However, the hypothetico-
deductive method consists simply of setting up premises and deduc-

[6]

ing consequences from these. All the methods of explanation examined so far have this in common. Is the term applied to distinguish these theories from explanations working from no premises and coming to conclusions without the processes of deduction?

Second, it should be noted that both these types of explanation, the generalizatory and the structural, can be expressed in mathematical notation, or be quantitatively stated. This is important, as lately a hybrid beast, called the mathematical model, has been introduced to add to the welter of names which comprehend too much. To say that an explanation or model is mathematical is not to say anything about what type of explanation it is, but only to specify what language has been used in its expression. Boyle's law can be stated mathematically and so can the kinetic theory of gases, but they still explain the same facts in a different kind of way. One is still an explanation in terms of the general case and the other still an explanation in terms of a structure. The introduction of quantities or symbolism does not alter the logical status of a theory.

The third type of theorizing, which some have claimed is of the structural rather than of the generalizatory type, is that involving hypothetical constructs (as opposed to intervening variables). It has been mentioned above when discussing Hull's notion of intervening variables that to say something is unobservable is too loose a criterion of classification, for things may be unobservable for various reasons. One may be that there really is nothing to observe beyond that which has been observed already. The so-called intervening variable may be the name of a disposition. Or it may be that things are inaccessible to observation in such a way that better methods of observation, such as microscopy, would render them visible. Mac-Corquordale and Meehl make this distinction very clearly. Speaking of intervening variables they say:

> Concepts of the first sort seem to be identifiable by three characteristics. First, the statement of such a concept does not contain any words which are not reducible to the empirical laws. Second, the validity of the empirical laws is both necessary and sufficient for the "correctness" of the statements about the concept. Third, the quantitative expression of the concept can be obtained without mediate inference by suitable groupings of terms in the quantitative empirical laws.

[7]

Speaking of hypothetical constructs they say:

> Concepts of the second sort do not fulfil any of these three conditions. Their formulation involves words not wholly reducible to the words in the empirical laws; the validity of the empirical laws is not a sufficient condition for the truth of the concept, inasmuch as it contains surplus meaning; and the quantitative form of the concept is not obtainable simply by grouping empirical terms and functions.

These hypothetical constructs require, according to MacCorquordale and Meehl, the existence of entities. These constructs should be "in correspondence with the actual events underlying the behavior phenomena." Though this distinction does something to sort out the heterogeneous entities—all labeled intervening variables or symbolic constructs by Hull—it still fails, in the writer's opinion, to achieve a satisfactory classification. As examples of what is meant by a hypothetical construct, MacCorquordale and Meehl give such entities as atoms, electrons, Hull's $r_g s$ (antedating goal reactions), $S_d s$ (drive stimuli), and afferent neural interaction. They also consider Hull's conditioning theory as in some way falling in the category of hypothetical constructs. "We suspect that Professor Hull himself was motivated to write these articles because he considered that the hypothetical events represented in his diagrams may have actually *occurred* and that the occurrence of these events represents the underlying truth about the learning phenomena he dealt with."

The classification, though apparently different, follows the same criteria as Hull's. There is a distinction according as something is actually observed or not. There is disagreement with Hull only about what is observed and what is not. Some of Hull's original intervening variables are classed as actual observables because they are symbolically equivalent to them. MacCorquordale and Meehl use the same basis for distinguishing various theoretical entities but show more logical sophistication in applying Hull's notions. Unfortunately the fundamental idea of distinguishing between various theoretical entities by their practical accessibility to observation does not seem to be sound. The mechanism of a clock is related in the same way to its behavior as the neural mechanism of an animal to the behavior which psychologists attempt to explain. Yet one

[8]

type of mechanism is directly observable, the other not, but this should not make a logical difference.

Alternatively MacCorquordale and Meehl's distinction can be thought of as arising from the application of two heterogeneous criteria. The first is: Is something, which is in principle observable, observable or unobservable in practice? This is an empirical criterion. The second is: How is a word, used in an explanation, related to the propositions which are to be explained? This second is a logical question. As a result MacCorquordale and Meehl's classification is unsatisfactory, as it leads to a confounding of the following two important logically distinct classes which both happen to be unobservable.

The first we may call hypothetical variables (dependent or independent), the other structural constructs. The first class has been already discussed above under the rubric of generalizatory explanation. It will be recalled that one of the developments of this method of explanation occurs when the laws stating the observed association of various events are extended to cases where some of these events are not observable. This kind of method is like that employed by the detective. By observing various regular conjunctions of classes of behavior he argues from the presence of one class which he can observe to the existence of the other which the criminal has been at pains to hide. In the same way, Hull, observing certain regularities between stimuli and responses, argues to the presence of stimuli, for instance drive stimuli, when he observes certain responses. A similar procedure is followed in the case of antedating goal reactions. In this type of case Hull extrapolates by assuming that a correlation which he has observed also exists where direct observation has not yet confirmed its existence. He therefore assumes that certain independent variables are present merely on the basis of other dependent ones, or vice versa. It should be clear that Hull's antedating goal reactions are in the same class as other reactions and that they are dependent variables which are hypothetical and that drive stimuli are hypothetical antecedent conditions. The fact that they have not been observed renders them hypothetical. This is not a logical property. Logically, they function the same way in Hull's explanations as other stimuli and antecedent conditions or as other dependent variables. They are therefore not hypothetical constructs but simply variables which are hypothetical (see Fig. 1).

The second, completely different type of thing, to which the label

[9]

hypothetical construct could apply is an element in a structural explanation. In such a class would come electrons, atoms, molecules, which are not merely unobserved instances of the class of phenomena to explain which they were postulated. A molecule in the kinetic theory of gases is not just an unobserved pressure, temperature, or volume. It is not an unobserved subclass of the classes which have been found to be related in a certain way. It is the constituent of a system which produces, or is held to produce, the phenomena which we observe and seek to explain. It is something like a cog in a calculating machine or a cell in the nervous system. It may not be unobserved. Its status is determined by its relationship to the phenomena which we are attempting to explain. That is why it need not be hypothetical, though it usually is. However, it can never do any job of explaining on its own. It only works as a part of a system and

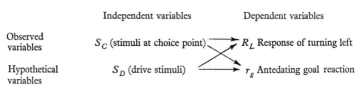

FIG. 1.—Part of a Hullian explanatory diagram. The diagram shows that variables which are logically the same (either independent or dependent) may yet be observationally different (observed or hypothetical) and vice versa.

that is why it is better to classify types of explanation than the entities of which they are composed. Electrons or atoms can hardly be said to have any meaning outside the systems in which they are elements—much less any explanatory power. There are, therefore, two types of hypothetical construct in MacCorquordale and Meehl's sense—those occurring in explanations of the generalizatory type and those functioning as elements in structural explanations.

It is perhaps because psychological explanations have been logically so mongrel that attention has been focused on the logical status of the constituents or entities composing them. The present writer believes that this is a mistake and that much of the speculation regarding these entities has obscured the essential problem of distinguishing between various types of explanation.

The two stages of a structural explanation.—An animal's behavior is produced by certain structures of which the organism is composed. An explanation of its behavior may be sought by specifying those structures or systems which produce its behavior. Ideally, if we knew an animal's physiology and anatomy in great detail and also knew the way the environment acted on detailed structures, we should be able to explain in a satisfying manner why, given certain conditions, the animal behaved in the way it did.

This is "explanation" in a sense which differs radically from the previous type, that of subsumption under a certain generalization about behavior. The former is an explanation in terms of other behavior of a like nature, the latter explanation in terms of observations or hypotheses about the underlying structure.

This second kind would seem more fruitful in psychology, as in science generally. We are observing the operations of a mechanism. If we knew what this mechanism was, the "generalization" type of explanation would be rather secondary and derivable from the structural type of explanation. This means that it would be possible to deduce logically the behavior of a mechanism whose structure we knew. On the other hand it would not be possible to deduce the structure of a mechanism by knowing its behavior. We could merely infer it. There are always many mechanisms consistent with a certain specific behavior. The statement about the mechanism plays the role of a hypothesis. The hypothesis entails the conclusions which it is called upon to explain; the conclusions do not entail the hypothesis. That is why the physiologist is in theory able to deduce certain overt behavior by studying the mechanism and why the psychologist cannot do the reverse. This may sound rather pessimistic. It looks as if the student of behavior can never provide an explanation of his own observation. This, however, is too hasty a conclusion from the argument. Merely because he cannot deduce the mechanism does not mean that he cannot form hypotheses about it. He may still be able to infer, although he cannot deduce. The hypotheses about the mechanism which are thus put forward will tend to entail statements about the behavior of an animal which have not been tested. If these predictions turn out to be correct this strengthens the hypothesis. If they are false, the theory tends to be refuted. Though psychologists as students of behavior cannot put forward hypotheses of absolute certainty, they can make suggestions whose plausibility may be enhanced or lessened by experiment.

To this type of procedure the objection can be made that it involves the creation of physiological mythology; for to suggest physiological mechanisms without direct observational warrant for their existence is fanciful. There is a great deal of substance in this objection but it cannot be treated as an objection to all kinds of attempts to arrive at a structural explanation. It applies only to a particular type of speculation—that which cannot in principle be checked by observations undertaken on the behavior of the animal as a whole or, in other words, the type of observations normally made by psychologists. These speculations concern the embodiment of the system employed. For instance, to attempt to guess at the particular change which occurs in the central nervous system during learning in the framework of a theory purporting to explain behavior is not only unnecessary but also purely speculative. That some type of change occurs may be inferred from the behavior of an animal. What this type of change is cannot be arrived at, nor is it very important for the psychologist to know. This can be shown by taking the example of an insightful learning machine (chap. x). To be told that the semipermanent change in the machine which occurs when it learns is due to a uniselector arm coming to rest does not help us to understand the behavioral properties of the machine. Nor can it be checked by performing experiments on the behavior of the machine. For the change could equally well be due to a self-holding relay, a dekatron selector, or any type of gadget known to technology capable of being turned from one steady state into another. In the same way to speculate about terminal end boutons in the way that Hebb does or about changes of synaptic resistance seems to be trying to answer a question irrelevant, strictly speaking, to the psychological theorist. What behavior would one of these assumptions explain which the others would not?

This would seem a good argument against speculating about the mechanism underlying behavior, but not against attempting to infer the type of mechanism or the system producing behavior. Clearly, the question about what the actual physical change is which occurs during learning in the machine is the wrong type of question to ask and to attempt to answer. For, whatever the answer, we still do not understand how the machine learns. Nor if we hazard a guess about it can we verify it, if we are restricted to observing the machine's behavior. Information about the physical identity of the parts of the machine sheds an extraordinarily feeble light on the explanation of the machine's capacities. It is about as useful as a map of the disposition of its parts in space, the pursuit of the knowledge of which in the animal is the preoccupation of much of physiological psychology. Now there is a tendency to argue that, since it is not profitable

[12]

to speculate about the physical properties of the parts of a machine and, since a machine is made up of physical parts, it is not profitable to speculate about the machine at all. Hence, it is advocated that we should seek only to construct general statements about behavior and leave what produces it to the physiologist.

Thus it appears that theoretical psychology must either do too much or too little. According to one school of thought we must only redescribe in a more economical manner. According to the other school we must either wait for physiology and anatomy or dream up our own. However, there appears to be a third possibility. It may be brought out if we again consider the example of the insightful learning machine. It was stated above that the change which occurs in learning in the machine could be engineered in many different ways. Any component which could be made to assume either of two steady states could be used. Similarly, the rest of the "central nervous system" could be constructed of completely different types of components without affecting the behavioral capacities of the machine. The precise properties of the parts do not matter; it is only their general relationships to each other which give the machine as a whole its behavioral properties. These general relationships can be described in a highly abstract way, for instance, by the use of Boolean algebra. This highly abstract system thus derived can be embodied in a theoretically infinite variety of physical counterparts. Nevertheless, the machines thus made will have the same behavioral properties, given the same sensory and motor side. Therefore, if we wish to explain the behavior of one of these machines, the relevant and enlightening information is about this abstract system and not about its particular embodiment. Further, given the system or abstract structure alone of the machine, we can deduce its properties and predict its behavior. On the other hand, the knowledge that the machine operates mechanically, electromechanically, or electronically does not help us very much at all.

An example based on this principle may be taken from an application of Boolean algebra to switching circuits by Shannon. In order to work out problems concerning switching systems, he uses a calculus exactly analogous to the calculus of propositions in symbolic logic. Each switching element is regarded as being either "open" or "closed," just as propositions in logic are either "false" or "true." From the symbolic interrelations of the elements can be deduced the properties of the network acting as a whole. Such expressions as

$0.0 = 0$ (a closed circuit in parallel with a closed circuit is a closed circuit) or $1 + 0 = 1$ (an open circuit in series with a closed circuit is an open circuit) clearly make no reference as to how any circuit is closed or opened or what the physical counterpart is of being in series or in parallel. Yet it is from manipulating expressions such as these that the properties of complex switching systems may be deduced. We do not need to know the physical identity of the elements of the calculus in order to be able to design systems to perform a set of operations or to display a certain type of behavior. We do not need to know the empirical content of a set of propositions in order to decide whether a given argument is valid. All we need to know is the truth or falsity of each proposition and the way the propositions are connected.

Now this argument is not directed against physiological knowledge; for direct observational evidence about the workings of a system whose properties we must normally infer is valuable. From observations on accessible parts we may glean valuable hints or corroborating evidence about the type of organization which it would be plausible to infer. An example of this may be found in the relation of Burns's work on cortical propagation to the type of system postulated for form recognition (chap. xi). On the other hand, it is an argument against the necessity for a certain type of physiological speculation in which many psychological theorists have felt themselves obliged to indulge. There has been no clear distinction between that part of an explanation of behavior which can be expressed as an abstract system and the identification of the elements of this system in terms of actual physical counterparts. The foregoing analysis has tried to make it clear that it is possible to separate these two steps. Once the distinction is clear it becomes fairly obvious that a psychologist need only speculate about the system and not its embodiment. It is not incumbent upon a theorist to suggest what is the embodiment of his hypothesis; a complete specification of its embodiment would add very little to the explanatory power of his system.

These two stages of explanation should be recognized as being separate. The purely intellectual aspect of the confusion of a system with its embodiment is lamentable enough, but the practical consequences are even worse. The theorist infects his critics with the confusion, and explanations tend to be rejected because their author made a faulty guess about the embodiment of the system he put

[14]

forward. This threatens to be the fate of Köhler and Wallach's theory of figural aftereffects. Here the system has been put by Köhler into a certain electrophysiological fancy dress and his critics have concentrated on tearing this to pieces under the impression that they were disposing of the explanation.

Another consequence of the failure to keep these two stages of explanation separate is a loss of rigor in the systems which really do the main job of explaining. An air of precision is lent to the author's system by detailed physiological identification of its elements, an endeavor inspired by the mistaken belief that we cannot understand how a mechanism works unless we know the identity of its parts. Meanwhile, the system which is the crux of the explanation is never clearly stated, disguised as it is in its identification, and would not do the job with which it was credited, however we chose to interpret it physically.

The fact that a system can be interpreted in various ways has some interesting consequences. First, it is possible to express a theory in terms of a model by giving it an identification which is already familiar and thus easier to think about than a completely abstract system. The identification is here a mere psychological aid and does not add or detract from the explanatory value of the system itself. This is often not understood. For instance, Lehrman in a recent article attacks the Tinbergen-Lorenz theory, which uses hydraulics to clothe its system on the grounds that no hydraulic arrangements have been found in the central nervous system.

Second, machine models of a system can actually be made by choosing appropriate physical counterparts. These will then display the behavior which the system was designed to explain. If the original system was complicated enough the physical model will "compute" the predictions to be made from it. The endeavor to make a model may also reveal inadequacies in the theory. It is impossible to make a machine work by wishful thinking. It is, however, only too easy to gloss over theoretical inadequacies on paper. Further, the construction of a machine gives some measure of the simplicity and economy of a system.

But perhaps the greatest benefit to be derived from the construction of actual machine models is a practical one. The fabrication of a concrete model gives a far more vivid insight into the relation between structure and behavior. It provides an experience of inestimable intellectual value for the psychologist, especially as it is one which cannot be satisfactorily conveyed verbally.

[15]

CONCLUDING CONSIDERATIONS

What implications have these points for the construction of psychological theory? Most psychologists would agree that the behavior of an animal is produced by some underlying physiological structure. Now even though it has been agreed that it is impossible to infer the complete details of this mechanism, the possibility remains that we can attempt to construct theories about the type of machine operating. That is, it might still be feasible to formulate a more general hypothesis but one which would reconstruct the more important, albeit more abstract, design of the mechanism whose external behavior we observe. There would thus be a middle road between the absurdities of the pseudo-physiologist and the sterility of positivism run wild.

The argument which is put against this type of hypothesis construction is that we can never know that we are right and, therefore, by implication, any attempt to make such theories is worthless. Here again, in this objection there is no appreciation of the limited objectives of scientific procedure. Merely because we cannot have absolute certainty—and this is true of any scientific belief—it does not mean that we must renounce any beliefs whatsoever. We can be content with adopting the ones which on the evidence appear to be the most plausible. In any case, it is unlikely that any hypothesis in psychology can at present be of more than a provisional nature. It should be sufficient that a theory leads to further predictions concerning the outcome of experiments which have not yet been performed. In this way it will be possible to establish precisely in what way the present theories do not fit the facts and to use experiment to narrow the range of theoretical possibility. It is difficult to envisage an ordered scientific advance in any other way. The number of possible experiments that can be performed is infinite. Without some sort of policy which leads to a narrowing of theoretical possibilities, experiments proliferate chaotically. Of facts there is already too much in psychology, of evidence too little.

II

The Hullian and the Tinbergen-Lorenz Theories of Need

A word of caution is necessary at this point to forestall a possible criticism. It might be objected that words like "need," "insight," "learning" are used in this book without a proper definition and that a definition is necessary before we can go on to formulate theories about these subjects. It should be clearly understood that no attempt is made to explain need, learning, or insight, but only the behavior of animals under various conditions. Terms like need, learning, and insight are used only as abbreviated ways of referring to the animals' behavior under various conditions and not as the causal agents. Their function is to indicate to the reader roughly what class of experiments conventionally collocated under a chapter heading in textbooks is to be discussed at any particular point. Therefore the meanings of these words do not have to be defined precisely in advance. Indeed, if they were, they would lose much of the usefulness they possess—somewhat like the British Commonwealth.

This chapter is devoted to a discussion of some of the main theories of need at present in vogue. These are critically examined in the light of the experimental evidence on the subject. The first to be examined is that of Hull, who has in this part of his theory come nearest to providing an explanation in terms of a mechanism. Briefly, Hull considers that certain physiological conditions in the animal stimulate peripheral receptors. "Organisms require on the whole a rather precise set of conditions for optimal chances of individual and species survival. When those conditions deviate appreciably from the optimum, a state of need is said to exist, and a more or less persistent stimulation (S_D) arises" (Hull, 1951, p. 15). "When a

[17]

need stimulates a receptor the resulting afferent neural impulse proceeds toward the central ganglia which act as a kind of 'automatic switchboard' directing the impulse to the muscles or glands whose action is necessary to reduce the particular need." So far Hull's position is explicit. However, we are left to infer that the activity provoked by this stimulation is shut off when the need ceases. We are told that the drive stimuli are reduced by certain movements. "In case none of these responses diminishes the need, the organism may die or fail to reproduce. . . . If, however, any of the evoked movements chances to reduce the receptor discharge characteristic of a need (S_D), the stimuli and the stimulus traces at that time acquire an increment of connection. . . ." The stimuli appear to continue while the need persists.

We thus have a system of the following type. A physiological change causes afferent stimulation. The afferent stimulation provokes effector activity, and this activity terminates the need. The termination of the need will then indirectly lead to a cessation of responding.

This theory can be tested in various ways. We can, for instance, attempt to alter the relation of the afferent stimulation to the need by removing the structures which are presumably stimulated by the need. The stomach's contraction in hunger has been thought to generate afferent impulses which in turn cause eating. The abolition of such impulses by gastrectomy has been found neither to eliminate eating nor to modify hungry behavior beyond what might be expected as a mechanical or clinical consequence of such an operation (Tsang, 1938; Bash, 1939). A related test of the hypothesis is to intensify or imitate any effect which the need has on the structures which supposedly generate the drive impulses. This has been done in the case of thirst, where dehydration is allegedly responsible for a dryness of the throat. Various types of interference with the flow of saliva have failed to increase the total water intake (Montgomery, 1931). Of course, it can be said that the wrong organs have been operated upon and that these experiments do not disprove Hull's hypothesis. They still render it less plausible, especially as similar results have been obtained in the case of mating (Beach). Here it has been possible to remove all the genital structures without a diminution of copulatory attempts, provided that the supply of appropriate hormone was artificially maintained.

Another less equivocal way of testing the hypothesis is to estab-

[18]

lish the temporal relationship between the cessation of activity and the termination of a need. We should on Hull's theory expect a close contiguity between these two events. Such a contiguity is of course suspect on general grounds. For instance, eating stops long before the processes of digestion are complete. It is difficult to see that any physiological state is restored in the process of mating. (It is true that Hull speaks of conditions for optimal chances of individual and species survival and their deviation from the optimum, but the deviation from the optimum for the species must presumably correspond to some change in the individual.)

More direct experimental evidence has been provided by Bellows (1939). He found that a thirsty dog with an esophageal fistula drank a certain amount and then ceased, even though no water had reached the animal's stomach. The deviation from the optimum had not been corrected. A possible defense for Hull against the validity of this evidence would be to say that the animals had simply learned by a process of trial and error when they had drunk enough. A similar argument could be employed in the case of eating. However, there are two arguments against this: the first from his theoretical premises and the other from one of his own experiments (Hull et al., 1951). Hull assumes that any stimulus will tend to evoke a response, provided that they have occurred together in close conjunction with a drop in the motivational stimulus (S_D). Thus the stimulus-response combinations which will be most strongly reinforced in the case of eating and drinking will be those which occur after the processes of assimilation have begun to take place. Thus the continuance of eating and drinking all the time the digestion is operating should be assured also on this further Hullian principle. In any case if the dog is behaving the way it does while it has an esophageal fistula merely because it has learned from previous experience that a particular amount of drinking will remedy its water deficit, we should expect such learning to be also manifest when it is eating under the same circumstances. However, Hull et al. (1951) have shown that this is not so. A dog will ingest a great deal more than its normal requirement when no food reaches its stomach. Early in this experiment, the dog concerned ate about 8 kg. of food before stopping for 5 minutes, though he weighed only 10 kg. before his operation.

It therefore seems that even if we were to alter Hull's postulates to enable him to predict a lack of coincidence between the cessation of a consummatory activity and the cessation of a physiological imbalance, an explanation in terms of learning would hardly be open to him. For he would still have to explain the discrepancy between drinking and eating.

If the above arguments are correct, Hull's difficulties as shown by the experimental evidence are twofold. The first is that he assumes that the consummatory act coincides in its duration with the physiological state which initiated it. It is certainly true, as will be shown later, that the initiation and maintenance of activities like eating, drinking, and mating are dependent on various physiological factors. But these activities do cease independently of these physiological factors once they have begun.

The second of Hull's difficulties stems from his assumption that specific peripheral stimuli initiate and maintain consummatory activities and that their cessation leads to a termination of these activities. It is held by the present writer that the opposite is the case. Stimuli do not evoke these responses, they terminate them. The arguments for this view will be presented in the next chapter.

A modification of Hull's theory which has been espoused by Miller is that it is the diminution of the drive stimuli produced by the physiological need which produces a diminution of such activities as eating. It is held that these stimuli, produced by the need, can cease before the need itself has disappeared. However, some of the arguments urged against Hull still apply—for instance, that the evidence for drive stimuli is very thin. Other criticisms are not applicable, but this seems to be because the theory is somewhat circular. Behavior is held to cease when drive stimuli cease, and drive stimuli are held to cease when behavior ceases. There is no independent criterion for establishing the cessation of drive stimuli except the cessation of driven behavior. Accordingly, if we grant the presence of drive stimuli in spite of the evidence against them, the theory says very little.

The Tinbergen-Lorenz hypothesis avoids these assumptions of Hull but runs into difficulties of its own. This theory assumes that there is a center which is loaded or charged up by various factors, such as hormones and perhaps some peripheral stimuli. The stored accumulation is then discharged through efferent pathways and gives rise to consummatory activity in proportion to the amount stored. The discharge takes place when a particular stimulus arrives. The stimulus thus causes only the onset of the consummatory activity, its duration being determined by the previous activity of a "need" on the center. The motor activity can thus cease independently of the original need and yet be to some extent proportionate to it. Such a notion is certainly more sophisticated than Hull's and is not implausible. It is supported, for instance, by some of the observations of Bellows, quoted above. Bellows found that dogs with an esophageal fistula would drink only approximately the amount of water which they would have done had water been entering their stomach. However, the chief difficulty with the theory is that on it the amount of past "need" or charging-up should correlate with the amount of effector activity during the consummatory act. Such a deduction is contradicted by Kohn's experiment (1951). This worker trained rats in a Skinner box to press a lever for a small amount of nutrient solution. He took the rate of lever pressing as a measure of drive. After the animals had been taught this habit, some of them had a quantity of the reward solution introduced directly into the stomach. Their rate of lever pressing declined very appreciably, in contrast with one of the other groups which had had saline introduced into the stomach instead. Berkun, Kessen, and Miller (1952) confirmed this result using a different criterion of drive reduction. In their experiment the amount of food ingested by the animal after the nutrient solution had been inserted served as a measure of drive.

However, the interpretation of these experiments can be called in question. The fact that animals ate less after the injection of the nutrient solution could be due to nausea, although the results obtained from the group treated similarly with saline would argue against this. To exclude such objections even more completely, Miller and Kessen undertook another experiment. These authors argue that if this procedure produced nausea it should produce avoidance. On the other hand, if it was genuinely "drive reducing," it ought to have a reward value and animals should learn to run toward the place where this procedure took place. They therefore taught an animal to run a T-maze in which the solution was artificially inserted in the stomach in one of the arms. The animals after they had learned this turned into this arm. Such a finding seems inconsistent with the explanation that such a procedure induces nausea.

Thus it seems that it is the actual entry of food into the stomach which leads to a cessation of eating. The animal's disposition to eat can be terminated without any efferent activity to speak of. That entry of food into the stomach is the important factor in ending eating activity and not the amount of eating activity itself has been shown in another way by Hull *et al.* (1951). These arranged the opposite experiment. They allowed a dog with an esophageal fistula to feed. They found as reported above (p. 19) that the animal would continue to swallow food far in excess of its normal requirements.

It could of course be said that the theory fits the case of drinking and that the mechanism of eating may be a special category. There are, however, elements even in drinking behavior itself which cast suspicion on the Tinbergen-Lorenz explanation. For instance, Bellows (1939) found that if a sufficient amount of water is introduced artificially into the stomach of the animal and the animal is not allowed immediate access to water, it will drink progressively less and less the later it is allowed to drink and that after approximately 15 minutes it will not drink at all. The stored accumulation of "energy" appears to have been dissipated without any drinking movements. The theory is therefore also unsatisfactory here.

Though the writer regards the above criticisms as cogent, he feels that his treatment of these theories may throw a less favorable light on them than they deserve. Both of them are part of broader theories. These wider hypotheses were designed with other bodies of evidence primarily in mind. The small segments of these theories examined above were probably constructed as extrapolations from the main body of larger hypotheses. They may be regarded as extensions in harmony with a broader framework. To take these fragments in isolation when criticizing them emphasizes their faults without sufficiently evoking the plausibility which they gain from their context.

III

A Suggested Mechanism of Need

It is often said that the time is not ripe for the formation of theories in psychology.* The seemingly contradictory evidence in the field of motivation, some of which has been mentioned, might lend color to such a view. On the other hand, there is no a priori way of determining when the right stage for the framing of hypotheses has arrived. However, some reasons for waiting before we attempt to explain are given. The paucity of experimental data is sometimes alleged to make the building of theory impossible. This would not be a good reason even if there was a lack of available information. The fewer the facts, the more theoretical possibilities there are with which these are compatible; the easier it is, therefore, to suggest a model. It may of course not be the right one but this is no objection to a theory in advance; otherwise every theory would have to be dismissed before it was constructed. Others skeptical of theory construction say that we do not yet have a good measure of what we are attempting to explain. Those who argue this are often involved in the application to psychological data of systems of measurement somewhat misleadingly called "information theory." The usual purpose in measuring events in various ways is to discover regularities in them. But there is no dearth of observed regularities in the subject matter of psychology already. If we had a theory to explain these, we should also know what observations would test it and systems of measurement would accordingly suggest themselves. The development and application of complicated mathematical techniques of mensuration seems to be of dubious value when we have no hypothesis to test.

* The theoretical ideas contained in this and subsequent chapters (iii–xi) are a development of articles published by the author in the *British Journal of Psychology* (1953, 1956).

[23]

However, the doctrine that theories are premature is a convenient one for its exponents. It exonerates them from having to pay serious attention to existing attempts and saves them from the labor of rigorous thinking.

In the view of the present writer it is never too early to have an explicitly worked-out hypothesis. It seems well-nigh impossible to approach a body of evidence or an observation without hypotheses of some sort. Even those who claim that theories are premature generally possess a theory, but one which is vague and not really conscious. Therefore the danger which undoubtedly exists of reading one's prejudices into the data cannot be avoided by refusing to theorize. Such considerations, and the manifest inadequacies of previous theories on the subject, are the writer's excuse for putting forward his proposals.

It is postulated that there is a set of elements (assumed to be somewhere in the central nervous system) set into activity by, or sensitive to, a specific change or state of the fluid surrounding it. This is the case in hunger, thirst, mating, and instincts of a like sort. One of these postulated elements, each sensitive to different states, is held to be present for each of these activities. The element partly underlying male mating behavior may be sensitive to male sex hormones, that concerned with thirst is brought into activity by cellular dehydration, and so on. The exact chemical identification of these states is, of course, unimportant to the theory qua system and need only be made tentatively.

When these central structures are excited, they indirectly excite a portion of the motor system, causing the animal to persist in a certain type of activity. (This will be dealt with more fully in the next chapter.) This activity produces a particular receptor (analyzer) discharge. This discharge from the analyzer is transmitted back to the central structures, depressing their excitability or sensitivity to the particular state which excites them (see Fig. 2).

The notion that there are actually components of the central nervous system sensitive to various fluctuations of conditions in the bloodstream has received some recent physiological support. Verney (1947) has inferred the existence of osmoreceptors "somewhere in the vascular bed normally supplied by the internal carotid artery." Andersson (1953) by injecting hypertonic saline into some parts of the hypothalamus of goats was able to produce drinking behavior. In case it is felt that he may have merely been causing

[24]

primarily diuresis of which drinking was but a mechanical consequence, he does report that the thirsty behavior occurred some of
the time without accompanying diuresis. Further warrant for
separating the mechanism of diuresis is provided by Barker, Adolph,
and Keller. They found that though some lesions caused both
exaggerated drinking and exaggerated urinary flow, sectioning of
the pituitary stalk caused exaggerated drinking alone. There is
therefore evidence for some sort of central structure sensitive to
cellular dehydration.

A direct confirmation of the theoretical postulation of a center
sensitive to dehydration and linked with drinking behavior has
recently been provided by Miller (1957). Using Andersson's technique of injecting fluid directly into some parts of the hypothalamus,
he was able to increase drinking behavior by injecting tiny amounts

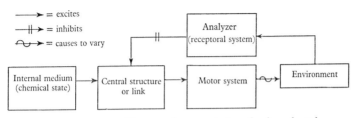

Fig. 2.—Diagram to illustrate the suggested mechanism of need

of hypertonic solution. By injecting the same amount of pure water
in the same position, drinking could be reduced in a thirsty animal.
If the injection was of isotonic saline, no difference was produced.

Andersson and McCann (1955) have also found that electrical
stimulation of the hypothalamus of the goat in the region dorsal to
the infundibular between the fornix and the tract of Vicq d'Azyr,
just lateral to the paraventricular nucleus and midway between the
dorsal and ventral hypothalamus, elicits drinking. These same authors (1956) found that lesions in this area in dogs abolish or very
much reduce water intake. Further, Greer (1955) has found that repeated stimulation of a part of the hypothalamus in the rat can
cause water intakes of up to 400 cc. in 24 hours.

It appears that a center similar to that for thirst also exists for
hunger. Smith (1956) has found that electrical stimulation of the
lateral hypothalamus greatly increased food intake. Anand and
Brobeck (1951) found that, after lesions in the same area of the

hypothalamus, animals die from starvation. Such evidence provides good support for a part of the hypothesis put forward.

It has already been stated that each of these central structures is thrown into activity for as long as a particular chemical change lasts. This statement must now be qualified in one important respect. Each of these elements—or primary links, as they will be called—is innately connected to a receptoral structure, which, when switched on, terminates the link's activity. This means that each primary link will receive afferent impulses which will turn it off. The primary link sensitive to cellular dehydration is in all probability connected to receptors in the mouth and throat, the links mediating some of the special appetites to taste receptors, and the primary link underlying hunger partly to taste receptors but mainly to receptors in the stomach. From the stomach the afferent message may be hormonal. These identifications are again tentative.

Direct neurophysiological techniques have given support to this hypothesis (which was first published in 1953 [Deutsch, 1953]). The hypothesis was an inference from the behavior of the animal to its structure. Some of this structure now appears to be uncovered. It appears that there are centers in the hypothalamus associated with feeding, whose function can be identified with that of the analyzer in the system put forward above. It has been found by Smith (1956) that electrical stimulation of the ventromedial nucleus in the hypothalamus caused hungry rats to reduce their food intake greatly. This is just what we would expect if the analyzer inhibiting the excitation of the central structure or link was itself being excited. It has long been known that a lesion in the ventromedial nucleus of the hypothalamus produces hyperphagia resulting in gross obesity. This hyperphagia would on the present theory be due to a removal of the analyzer responsible for signaling that food has arrived in the stomach. On this supposition we should expect that the animal should keep on eating every time the internal medium irritated the central structure or link until the internal medium ceased its irritation. This would be due to the absence of the message from the stomach to depress the irritability of this central structure or link. (The animal would in one way resemble the dog of Hull *et al.* with an esophageal fistula.) Indeed, it is found that the animal overeats grossly and if allowed unlimited access to food becomes extremely obese. Having reached a certain weight, it does not eat such large amounts any longer but still eats much more than a

[26]

normal animal, and it keeps its weight up. This is again what one would predict if one accepts the identification in terms of the present hypothesis. When food from the internal medium can no longer be stored away as fat tissue, the level of the internal medium will only fall sufficiently to irritate the central structure when metabolic processes deplete it. Though the irritation of the primary link by the fall in the level of the internal medium may be slight, if the animal has access to a supply of food, it will start to eat. In spite of the low level of excitation the animal will consume an abnormal amount, as the irritation of the primary link will not be reduced in the normal way by the firing of an analyzer. However, the eating behavior can easily be suppressed by other motivational factors because the excitation causing the eating is in fact low. Teitelbaum (1955) has demonstrated that this is the case for factors causing avoidance. Similar results have been reported by Miller, Bailey, and Stevenson (1950) on the rat and by Fuller and Jacobs (1955) on genetically obese mice. It is predicted that other factors causing approach should also interfere with eating in these animals in a similar way. It is also possible that the voracity of the hyperphagic animal after operation is due to the removal of a steady inhibition usually caused by the spontaneous firing in the ventromedial nucleus (which would be expected to increase when the animal is eating). Such an effect would manifest itself as equivalent to a sudden drop in the level of the internal medium.

So far the present theory has much in common with the two previously discussed, those of Hull and Tinbergen. Some physiological state is presumed to act upon a structure, peripheral in Hull's case and central in Tinbergen's. On the Tinbergen-Lorenz hypothesis the irritation is stored and the store released when the appropriate stimulus arrives. Hull believes that the irritation is transformed into motor activity directly when the relevant external stimuli arrive. The present theory resembles Hull's more closely on this point. The irritation is not stored but generates an activity only while it is present, to the extent of its intensity at each moment. However, the system differs radically from both theories in the role which the stimulus or afferent message plays in it. The firing of the receptoral organization attached to each primary link terminates its activity. As this excitation in the primary link is regarded as the cause of the animal's responses, it may be said that the stimulus terminates a response. This is in contrast to the previous theories

[27]

where the stimulus was given an exclusively exciting or releasing function. This damping of activity by the stimulus can be envisaged as being caused by an increasing desensitization of the primary link to the particular chemical state which irritates it into a state of excitation.

These notions may be restated in the following way. The primary link is set into activity by a particular chemical change which irritates it. The change in this feature of the internal environment irritates the primary link in proportion to the magnitude (or perhaps in some cases the rate) of this change. The primary link causes the motor organization to come into activity. When the receptoral system connected to a particular primary link fires off, the irritability of the primary link to the particular chemical change which set it off begins to decrease. Therefore, the time taken for the analyzer to decrease the irritability of the link by gradually raising the threshold of the link until a given amount of irritation becomes ineffective will vary with the amount of the irritation by the internal environment. Therefore, we should expect the amount of stimulation required for the animal to cease eating or drinking to be proportionate to the particular deficit. In the intact animal the amount ingested will correlate with the stimulation necessary to shut the activity off. Further, if the stimulation necessary to desensitize the primary link is applied artificially, activity will not take place at all. The cessation, or non-occurrence, of a motor activity like eating or drinking will result in spite of the continuance for some time or permanently of the chemical state which initiated the activity, and this is the case in the intact animal. For instance, in drinking, when the appropriate receptors have been stimulated to an extent sufficient to lead to a cessation of drinking, water must have entered the stomach. This water will then slowly redress the change which occasioned the drinking, comparatively long after drinking has ceased.

In the case of the animal with an esophageal fistula (Bellows, 1939) which is permitted to drink, we should expect the animal to stop drinking when the receptors in its mouth and throat have been sufficiently stimulated, even though no water had entered its stomach. However, as no water is being absorbed from the stomach while the animal sham-drinks (with no consequent lessening of the irritation of the primary link), the total amount sham-drunk should be somewhat larger than the amount drunk ordinarily. Also, as dehydration will persist and increase under these circumstances, the animal should begin to start drinking again as soon as the desensitization of the primary link has worn off sufficiently. Further, if water is inserted directly into the stomach of a thirsty animal, it should drink the same amount as if this had not been done. However, the amount ingested should decrease progressively with time as the irritation of the primary link due to dehydration decreases as the water finds its way from the stomach to the tissues. These are in essence the findings of Bellows.

Miller, Sampliner, and Woodrow found results which at first sight contradict those of Bellows. These workers found that water injected directly into the stomach of rats produced a prompt lessening of drinking behavior. There was also a reduction in the rate of bar-pressing for water. This result is parallel to the results found in hunger. It is also found that water ingested by mouth causes a greater diminution in thirst measured either by instrumental behavior (bar-pressing) or consummatory behavior (drinking). It seems, however, that the parallel between hunger and thirst as found in this experiment may be misleading. Miller and his collaborators should have investigated the rate of absorption of the water from the stomach. If this is governed by the ratio of volume of fluid to the surface area of stomach, then the rate of absorption should be much higher in the case of the rat than in the case of the dog, as the rat is a very much smaller animal. Consequently the dehydration of the tissues in the case of the dog would last much longer than in the case of the rat. Until this explanation in terms of the physical rates of absorption is tested and found false, it would seem preferable to regard the mechanisms of thirst in rats and dogs as analogous.

Studies on the rates of absorption of water from the gut may not have a good estimate of the relief of physiological water deficit. Wolf (1958, pp. 153–54) suggests that "unabsorbed water in the gut can take up systemic salt, possibly relieving thirst on an osmometric basis quite as if water had been absorbed." This process would also be much faster in the rat than in the dog.

Gastric distention has also been suggested as contributing to thirst satiation, e.g., Towbin (1949). Summarizing the results of various studies, Wolf (1958, p. 157) states: "Coupled with the findings of Towbin these results suggest that the inhibitory factor of distention in dogs exists, but that it operates only in extreme distention." It seems a priori unlikely that distention should play a part in the usual case, because distention with food would interfere with the drinking of adequate amounts of water.

In the case of hunger where the receptors are mainly to be found in the stomach, we should expect the same system to give rise to different behavioral consequences. For instance, the placing of food directly in the stomach should lead to an immediate cessation of eating activity as these receptors are stimulated. This contrasts with the case of thirst quoted above where the receptors responsible for the cessation of drinking are absent from the stomach and lie in the throat and mouth. That this deduction is correct has been experimentally shown. The rats in Kohn's (1951) investigation stopped lever-pressing when a nutrient solution was inserted directly in their stomach, before it could have had any appreciable effect on the chemical changes which occasioned that activity. Further confirmation of Kohn's results and the interpretation put on them by the present theory is to be found in experiments performed by Miller and Kessen (1952) and also by Berkun, Kessen, and Miller (1952). Moreover, it would be predicted that if an animal with an esophageal fistula was allowed to feed, it would continue to do so, if no food entered its stomach, to the point of physical exhaustion. The stimuli which normally shut this activity off would not be generated. Such an observation has been made by Hull *et al.* (1951).

That the stomach is capable of shutting off activity has been further demonstrated by Smith and Duffy (1955). These workers showed that the stomach responded with a considerable amount of discrimination in a way which would fit in with the role postulated for it in the present theory. They trained rats in a Skinner box to obtain food by pressing a bar. After training, their stomachs were filled with various substances through a stomach tube to determine the effects of these on the rate of bar-pressing. They found that non-nutritional bulk had no effect on the rate of lever-pressing. This was tested by injecting various amounts of kaolin mixture. However, when they injected a 30 per cent sucrose solution, which is nutritive, a depression of the rate of pressing occurred which was approximately linear with respect to quantity. Equal volumes of glucose and glycerol equiosmotic solutions had different effects. It therefore appears that the stomach does in some way discriminate and measure substances differing in bulk and quality.

Further evidence that it is the amount of afferent message generated by "consummatory" activity and not the activity itself which leads to a cessation of behavior has been obtained by Deutsch and Jones (1959). It was well known that rats, given both water and hypotonic saline solution, will drink much larger quantities of the saline. This behavior was generally ascribed to some kind of taste preference on the part of the rat. It was, however, interesting to note, from the point of view of the present theory, that Zotterman and his collaborators had shown that the signal for water and for salt traveled down the same nerve fiber in the case of the rat (and also, it seems, in the case of man). These signals are, however, differently coded. The water-salt fiber has a high rate of spontaneous firing. To signal water, the firing diminishes from the spontaneous level. A salty solution which is hypertonic is signaled by increase in the spontaneous rate of discharge.

As the decrease in the spontaneous rate of firing in the fiber seems to be brought about by the dilution in the fluids bathing the taste receptors, it would follow that hypotonic saline solution would cause less of a dilution per unit volume and therefore a smaller diminution in the rate of spontaneous firing. The amount of water signal generated by a certain volume of hypotonic saline would be smaller than that generated by an equal volume of water. If the animal's drinking persists until a certain quantity of "water" signal arrives, then we should expect the animal to drink more hypotonic saline than water. The saline would seem in a sense to be diluted water. Deutsch and Jones in fact found that, given equal and limited volumes of hypotonic saline and water as alternative rewards in a T-maze, the animals would learn to choose the water. This would not be expected if the animals' greater ingestion of saline was due to a preference and not to an effect of dilution. Hence, we can infer that it is the afferent signal generated by water which shuts off drinking because a diminution of this signal prolongs the duration of drinking and so increases the amount drunk.

Thus, whatever evidence later work may produce, it can be seen that the apparently irreconcilable and almost contradictory facts can be satisfactorily explained by an unitary hypothesis. The attempt to construct explanations would seem to be worthwhile.

Nevertheless the hypothesis put forward is restricted in its scope. It is not intended that it should be applied to the field of avoidance. It is meant only to cover activities or inborn tendencies which are appetitive. This limitation may best be seen if we consider the so-called special appetites. Deprivation of some essential substances leads the animal to show a preference for consuming these. In some cases such a preference has to be learned; this appears to be the case chiefly with substances which the animal cannot detect or taste (Young, 1948). These cases are outside the scope of the present hypothesis. The ingestion of these substances is presumed to be a consequence of an avoidance of symptoms associated with a deficit. Such a mechanism is also considered to operate in extreme cases of hunger and thirst where depletion is such that it gives rise to noxious stimulation. Such a mechanism was presumably operating in the experiment of Coppock and Chambers (1954).

The deprivation of other substances, such as salt, appears to give rise to an immediate appetite for the substance in question (Thomson and Porter, 1953; Epstein and Stellar, 1955). The mechanism in these cases is assumed to be homologous with that operating in hunger or thirst. The assumption here could be tested by offering the deficient animal a substance identical in taste with that of which the animal was deprived and which will not remove the specific deficit, previous learning having been excluded. Otherwise it is not possible entirely to remove the suspicion of some swift removal of noxious stimulation when the animal first tastes the needed substance. The animal ought to ingest the "dummy" substance in the same quantities, as measured by the stimulation produced, as its need-reducing counterpart.

Saccharin appears to be a dummy substance of this kind, at least in part. As has been suggested above, the primary link underlying hunger is connected partly to taste receptors but mainly to receptors in the stomach. Some of these receptors signal the arrival of sweet substances which are usually nutritive. Saccharin stimulates the receptors which signal the arrival of sugars, but it has no nutritive properties and presumably does not act on the stomach receptors. It should therefore be consumed in large quantities when the animal is hungry, and this is what Carper and Polliard (1953) have found. The message originating from it will be much smaller than from a solution which affects the stomach receptors too. A satiated animal drinking saccharin should be very like an obese hyperphagic eating food. The taste for sweet substances in general has a curious biological usefulness during foetal life. De Snoo (1937) demonstrated that the ingestion of amniotic fluid by the foetus during pregnancy plays an important part in regulating its amount and that apparently the foetus drank this fluid because of its sweet taste. He studied twenty pregnant women suffering from poly-hydramnios (a painful swelling of the abdomen owing to an excess of amniotic fluid). He thought that foetuses swallowed amniotic fluid in the normal case and that in these pregnancies it did not occur because the taste of the amniotic fluid was not right. He therefore injected saccharin, and in all twenty cases the abdomen went down. To check whether this effect was really due to the foetus drinking and not to some other effect of saccharin, he also injected methylene blue into the amniotic fluid. This substance appeared in the mother's urine after, but not before, he injected saccharin, and this confirmed his hypothesis.

There are some types of activity, like mating, where the level of the substance (like testosterone) which acts on the primary link is not affected by the performance of the act of copulation. There is only a diminution by the afferent message, deriving from orgasm, of the sensitivity of the primary link to the hormonal factor. The irritability of this primary link gradually recovers.

It is to be noted that the present system does not depend on some concept of "need" or deficit. The initial activity is caused by a feature of the internal environment acting on the primary link and causing it to fire until it is shut off by the firing of receptoral elements attached to it. The activity is brought to an end not by any alteration in deficit, "need," or any other alteration in the internal environment, though it may artificially be made to do so by this means. It is ended by the arrival of specific receptoral impulses. These may or may not be followed in the long run by a reversal of the state which initially caused the activity. Whether this is so or not depends not on any difference in the nervous mechanisms employed by the animal when manifesting these types of behavior but on other features of the animal's construction, such as its surgical intactness, or on its possession of a digestive tract. Hence it is wrong to regard the mechanism of "need" as a simple homeostat. Activity ceases before the change which caused it is reversed.

The system which has been postulated can be described in five propositions. There are five elements in it, related to each other in three different ways. The elements will be called an analyzer (a receptoral system); a link; a motor (or effector) organization; an environment; a feature of the internal environment. The three kinds of relation are activating; switching-off; causing to vary. The elements are related to form the unit in the following way:

[33]

1. The primary link is set into activity by a feature of the internal environment.

2. When the primary link is active it indirectly activates the motor organization.

3. The activity in the motor organization causes the environment to vary.

4. A particular variation of the environment activates the analyzer.

5. The activated analyzer switches off the link.

Most of these relations will not be all or none, but more or less in nature.

IV

*Innate and Acquired Behavioral
Sequences and Conflicts*

Often an animal executes a long and intricate series of movements
in order to secure the gratification which was discussed in the preceding chapter. A hypothesis was put forward concerning the unit
which underlies the final stage of appetitive behavior. To account
for the whole behavior sequence, such as the running of a maze,
this hypothesis must be extended. In order that the reader should
not become unduly perplexed by the more rigorous formulation
which follows, a loose sketch is first presented to enable him to
obtain an intuitive grasp of the system.

A behavior sequence, such as a rat's running a maze, is regarded
as a set of tropisms occurring in turn. First, the rat is attracted by
one feature or cue and then by the next, and so on until it reaches
the food in the goal. However, the rat is not always attracted by
those features. If it is not hungry, it will not run the maze. When it
is hungry, the cues in the maze become attractive. This is because
the units underlying these tropisms are connected together in such
a way that when the primary link in the system (described in the
preceding chapter) becomes excited, all the units underlying these
tropisms also become excited. When they become excited, the
"cues," triggering off the receptors attached to these units, will become attractive. The animal therefore "steers" toward any of
these cues which it picks up.

If two of the cues are picked up at the same time, the one which
is nearer the goal obtains precedence because of the way the excitation is transmitted from one unit underlying a tropism to the next.
The units are arranged in the order in which they occur with respect
to the goal (the primary link). One unit passes on excitation origi-

nating from the primary link to the next. But when its own receptor has been stimulated, the unit will cease transmitting this excitation and take over the "steering," as the cue which stimulates its own receptor will be attractive. The writer apologizes for the mentalistic overtones of this account, but such is the vocabulary which describes this type of behavior most economically. There is no harm in using these terms so long as we do not believe that their use explains the behavior they describe. If this is clear, there is no point in induging in laborious and obfuscatory periphrases.

Let us turn now to a more rigorous formulation. In the last chapter an element called a "link" was introduced.

1. This link was excited by features in the biochemistry of the surrounding tissues or fluids.

2. Now we shall suppose that there are also links in our system which are excited only by other links.

3. These links (as these elements are arbitrarily called) are connected to analyzers and motor outputs.

4. A primary link is not itself directly connected to the motor system. (The relation of the primary link to the motor output was not explicitly defined in the preceding chapter.) It is instead connected to a secondary link which receives its excitation from the primary link and is itself directly connected to motor output.

5. A secondary link is also connected to an analyzer. When such a link is receiving excitation from a primary link and stimulation from the analyzer, it will persist in exciting the same part of the motor system, and so maintain the same movement pattern, while the stimulation of it by the analyzer increases. When there is a decrease, its motor output will vary, and it will alter its movement pattern. A link will thus tend to maximize its own stimulation.

The writer has obtained some experimental evidence bearing on this point. It has long been known that when a singer is instructed to sing a steady note, the note sung is not steady but oscillates at a certain rate about the tone he is attempting to sing. This might be regarded as a muscular tremor often perhaps cultivated because it makes the voice sound richer. However, the writer formed the hypothesis that this tremor was due to the characteristics of the mechanism which controls movements and that it represented instead minute corrections of error when the voice strayed from the desired note. He therefore made subjects sing through a device which greatly amplified the volume of the voice and delayed its reception by the subject. When this occurs, the frequency of the subject's oscillations about the tone decreases. Also, the amplitude of the oscillations increases. This might be expected if the subject was indeed correcting what he was doing on the basis of what he heard (see also Deutsch and Clarkson, 1959a). Similarly, when pitch discrimination is artificially sharpened by an exaggeration of the heard change in pitch to the subject, the frequency of the oscillations increases. From these and similar experiments conducted by the author, it is concluded that each analyzer, such as that dealing with the reception of a particular pitch, fires to an increasing extent, the closer the correspondence to it of an incoming message. This rate of increase is picked up by a differentiating device. If the correspondence increases, the same action is further continued; if it decreases, the course of action is altered. Thus when we endeavor to maintain a certain pitch in singing, we correct when we hear that we are straying away from the set note and reverse our course of action when this last correction has begun to lead us into the opposite error and we perceive a decreasing correspondence with the note we aim to sing.

6. Returning again to the attachments of the secondary link, this secondary link may also be attached to another secondary link, to which it will transmit the excitation which it receives from another link (primary or secondary).

7. (a) This excitation will be transmitted only until the analyzer attached to the link is stimulated. The excitation present in this link will then be switched to control the motor system and the link will act to maximize its own stimulation by the analyzer (according to 5) (see Fig. 3). (b) Even when its analyzer has ceased to be stimulated, the link, which has stopped transmitting excitation because its analyzer was stimulated, will take some time before it will transmit excitation in the same proportion as before its analyzer was stimulated.

We thus have a system where the first link is connected to the second, the second to the third, and so on. The first activates the second, the second the third. Therefore, if the activity in the second ceases, it also ceases in the third. The first link, however, will remain active. The link is in effect just a switch, which conducts excitation this way or that, depending on the occurrence of a particular signal. A row of links is a set of switches arranged in series. Each of these switches has associated with it rather more complex

[37]

networks of switches, whose function is described in the rules and which it is convenient to regard also as parts of one link. The row of links is excited from its first member through each member in turn. (The first member underlies the aim last in time to the observer, e.g., feeding in the goal box in the maze.) If one of the members is stimulated by its analyzer, it will cease to transmit such excitation and begin to control the motor system in such a way as to maximize its own stimulation. In the course of this it will stimulate the analyzer of other links nearer the source of excitation and will thus itself be cut off from this source.

We thus have a system which will pursue aims in turn, in a predetermined sequence. When it has run through the sequence, it will cease to be active. For when it has achieved its final aim (our No. 1 in the sequence), there are no more activated links in the chain and therefore there is a cessation of output. We have here a hypothesis which enables us to look in the same way at performance both instinctive and learned. Even if no new prediction could be made on it, it would still be of value as a co-ordinating and unifying hypothesis. Second, this system will show a very interesting property. It will eliminate blind alleys or "superfluous" moves and break down on detour problems. This is deduced in the following way. Let us assume that a portion of a row composed of three links is activated with link No. 3 controlling output. If by chance the analyzer connected to No. 1 is fired off before the analyzer connected to No. 2, link No. 2 will not receive any more excitation from No. 1, nor will link No. 3. Link No. 1 will then control output. The system will not persist in pursuing an aim if that aim has been short-circuited, so to speak. If analyzer No. 2 is fired off by a cue up a blind alley, and analyzer No. 1 by a cue past the blind alley, the animal will not go up the blind alley but will pursue an aim nearer in order to the final goal. In some cases—that is in detour problems— the animal is allowed to see the goal but is not allowed to reach it except by pursuing aims which are now short-circuited by the firing-off of analyzers attached to links nearer in the row to the first, and it will therefore fail.

The activity in a row of links is transmitted by each member in turn from its first member. This first member is sensitive to changes in the internal medium and is set into activity by them, though its irritability to these changes decreases progressively as the analyzer which is connected to it is stimulated and the impulses from this message impinge on this link.

This first link in the chain will take some time before it resumes full irritability after being switched off. It will be in a refractory phase. Hence, this first member will take some time before it resumes activity, even though the internal medium may not change.

This relationship to the sensory message is different for the links other than the primary. Each link when it is active and exciting the motor system will persist in exciting the same part of the motor system and so the same movement pattern, while the input from the analyzer attached to this link increases. When there is a decrease, its motor output will alter. Perhaps the theory would become clearer if we gave an example of its application to a concrete instance; when a thirsty animal is running a maze for a reward of water, the following is assumed to occur. The "landmarks" in the maze are to be taken to be represented by analyzers arranged in the order in which the animal has found them on previous runs. The "cues" or "landmarks" nearest the goal are "represented" by analyzers connected to the link next in order to that excited by dehydration. Those cues at the entrance of the maze are farthest away on the row of links from this first link. When this first link is excited by dehydration, the whole row of links will be excited, link by link. The last link will in all probability be switched off without any activity on the part of the animal as the experimenter sets it at the entrance of the maze. For at this juncture it will see from a distance some other cue to which it will attempt to approximate itself. During this activity further cues will come into view, and as this happens the animal will locomote toward these. Any cue nearer the final goal will be selected rather than one farther away. For any analyzer which is set off by a cue nearer the goal will be attached nearer the first link from which the excitation in the row is originally derived. When this analyzer is set off, the link to which it is attached will cease transmitting excitation to its neighbor, so cutting it off from all the links farther away from the first link itself. In this way a clearly visible short cut will be taken as soon as it is introduced and blind alleys will be eliminated (see Figs. 3, 4, and 5).

The simple system which has been described can be regarded as having been set up either through learning or through genetic factors. It is assumed for the moment that the cues which set off the analyzers attached occur one after another. This involves an idealization, but one which works well enough in most situations. The complications ensuing when cues occur simultaneously are dealt with later, but they cause no great difference to the behavior of the system and need not worry the reader for the moment. It is interesting to compare this mechanism of behavior sequence with that of Tinbergen and Hull.

In Tinbergen's view behavior sequences are to be explained by

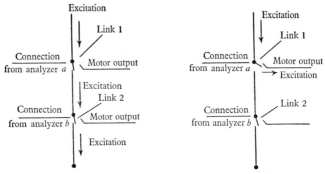

A. The flow of excitation before analyzer a is stimulated

B. The flow of excitation after analyzer a has been stimulated.

FIG. 3.—The effect of stimulating an analyzer on the flow of excitation. A link will transmit excitation to another link until the analyzer attached to it is stimulated. The excitation will then be switched to control the motor system.

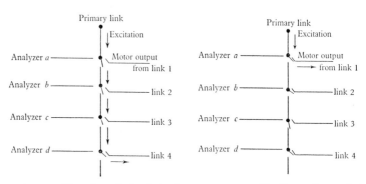

FIG. 4.—The effect of stimulation from two sources. The figure shows what happens when two cues, one farther from the goal than the other, occur. Stimulation from analyzer d is already occurring. Then analyzers a and b are stimulated and switch their two links to transmit to the motor output. When this occurs, only link 1 will be passing excitation to the motor output, as no excitation now travels past link 1. The system will therefore attempt to maximize stimulation from analyzer a.

[40]

reference to a hierarchy. A center is charged up by hormones, some stimuli, and the like and then discharges when a releasing stimulus occurs. Some of the stored energy is discharged through muscular action, and the rest drains to the next center, which is then loaded, ready to discharge when triggered by the next stimulus. On such a scheme the stimulus which arrives too early should produce no reaction. It will trigger a center which has not been loaded. Tinbergen (p. 47) quotes the example of the bee-hunting digger wasp (*Philanthus triangulum*) to illustrate this point. In this insect the

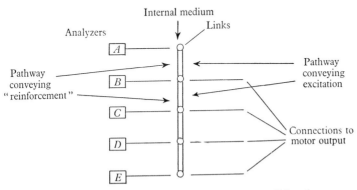

Fig. 5.—The system after learning has occurred. Two parallel pathways connect the links. One pathway conveys the excitation originating from the primary link. The other conveys information from one link to the next when their analyzers are fired in temporal proximity, which is what has led to their connection together in the first place, and to a lowering of "resistance" between them when such firing occurs again thereafter. Connection together can be thought of as the reduction of an extremely high "resistance."

smell of a bee will not be effective in producing a leap to seize the bee unless a previous reaction triggered only by seeing the bee has occurred. He then goes on to discuss the mating behavior of the three-spined stickleback as a "chain reaction of this type." (However, in fairness to Tinbergen, it should be mentioned that in a diagram on page 104 he seems to have a different scheme in mind. But it is difficult to know whether he wishes to explain the stickleback's behavior differently or whether he is using "the principle of hierarchical organisation" in a different way. Indeed, he uses this term to mean many different things.)

But the rigidity of the wasp is not a characteristic of the behavior of the stickleback, for whom this hypothesis was to a large extent designed. This appears from an incidental observation by Van Iersel. He tested the strength of the sex drive of the male three-spined stickleback by placing a female in a glass tube and presenting it to the male. He says: "The tube was always placed as far as possible from the nest in order to allow the male a full performance of the zig-zag dance. A female placed too near the nest does not release the zig-zag dance, but stimulates the male to show later parts of the courtship chain, viz., showing the nest entrance." Though his work is done in the context of Tinbergen's theory, he does not note the discrepancy here between his own observations and the theory with which he is working. On the other hand, such observations accord well with the view which has here been put forward. It is of course true that the view here put forward does not square with the behavior of the bee-hunting digger wasp, but it is perhaps not surprising that insects work on some principles which are not those to be found among the vertebrates.

Other difficulties for Tinbergen's hierarchical theory concern the using of the stored energy as the animal goes through a reaction chain. As the animal starts off with a more or less fixed amount of energy, which is built up only gradually, any excessive activity at one stage should use up more than its own quota of energy. This is especially difficult when there is an appetitive stage which has to be powered by the energy store. For instance, Tinbergen tells us that the female of the bee-hunting digger wasp *Philanthus triangulum* flies from flower to flower in search of a bee in the phase of the behavior where she is indifferent to the scent of bees. It is not clear at all what happens to the energy store if such searching is prolonged. We would expect on the theory as it stands that energy should be used up during this searching and that this should not leave so much for the other phases of the chain reaction. Consequently, we might expect the rest of the sequence to be weaker or to end prematurely. Such difficulties are avoided if we do not assume that a store of energy is being dissipated but that excitation persists while certain stimuli are missing.

Hull's system concerns itself chiefly with learned behavior. We shall therefore turn to a comparison after a description of how learning occurs on the present hypothesis. For, so far, the connections between the analyzer, link, and effector system have been regarded as fixed. This may be the case in the system underlying instinctive behavior. Here the variation in motor output may be largely absent too.

The system already outlined would not be capable of learning. The writer has supposed that there is a row or chain of links, each acting on others in the way described, with all the links already connected to analyzers and output units. It is supposed that such a structure underlies both innate and learned behavior. However, for innate behavior such a structure is present at birth; for learned behavior it must be built up.

It is supposed that prior to learning there are in the nervous system many units consisting of an analyzer connected to a link. This link is in its turn connected to the motor system. During the course of learning, the links become attached to each other to form the structure described above. This is done according to the following principle.

8. When there is a link whose analyzer is stimulated, another link, whose analyzer has just ceased to be stimulated, will be attached to the first link, so that this first link will transmit excitation to it.

Thus temporal succession of the stimulation of analyzers by cues will lead to an ordinal proximity of attachment when the row of links is formed. (This arrangement will be called links-in-series.) Therefore, when an animal is put in a maze and it sees cue a, which is then followed by cue b, then the link whose analyzer is set off by cue a will be attached to the link whose analyzer is set off by cue b. If cue b is then followed by the stimuli of food, then a similar connection will take place. As this food will be connected to a primary link, excited by a food deficit, the next time a food deficit occurs the primary link will be exited. This primary link will pass its excitation on to the food link, which will pass it to the cue b link, which will pass it on to the cue a link. Thus the whole row which has been formed will be excited. The animal, therefore, on being set down in the maze will seek out the cues according to the order in which they occurred in relation to the goal.

9. When there is a link whose analyzer is stimulated during the whole time the analyzer attached to another is being stimulated, then these two links will form an inhibitory connection. (This arrangement will be called "links in parallel.")

A link will diminish the excitation in other links through such

[43]

an inhibitory connection, such a relationship being reciprocal. This operates in the following way.

First, if links are connected in parallel, then the excitation flowing through each will be divided by the number of links connected in parallel, if they are connected only to each other and simultaneously excited.

Second, there will be some links connected in parallel and simultaneously excited, which are each connected in parallel to different numbers of other links, which may not be simultaneously excited, for instance when a cue occurs in two situations. Here an excited link will inhibit another excited link in inverse proportion to the number of other links connected together in parallel with it. Therefore a link with fewer parallel connections will conduct a larger proportion of the excitation. If, for instance, there are two connected in this way, one may conduct three-quarters of the excitation impinging on it, whereas the other may only conduct one-quarter because of the larger number of times its analyzer has fired off in combination with different analyzers.

In this way the excitation conveyed down a row of links will tend to be constant, regardless of the number of links in parallel at any one point. Hence, for most purposes of prediction we can assume that only a simple series arrangement is operating (by ignoring rule 9) with a complex cue at each point:

10. If there is only a partial overlap of the duration of two analyzers being stimulated, a series arrangement of the two links concerned will occur.

There are occasions when the sequence of environmental stimuli alters. Then one analyzer will not be succeeded by the firing of the analyzer next in the row.

11. After two links have been connected together, this connection will have a certain threshold of resistance to the flow of excitation. This threshold, or resistance, will be reduced each time the analyzers attached to these two links fire in succession in proportion to the amount of excitation of the links at the time and to the amount of firing from the analyzers.

12. This threshold of connection between two links will rise if link x, which is receiving excitation from the link y, is stimulated by its analyzer x and this is not succeeded by the firing of the analyzer y. And this threshold will continue to rise while this switching-off is delayed. This rise will be proportionate to the

amount of control of motor output by the link at the time. Thus where link y again receives excitation on a subsequent occasion, less will be passed to link x, and so to all the links which receive their excitation through x either directly or via the intermediacy of other links.

It is now possible to compare this system with Hull's on its ability to explain the experimental evidence.

It has been demonstrated by Hull (1951) and Leeper (1935) that rats can be taught to take one path to water when thirsty and another to food when hungry. Hull explained this by postulating two diverse persistent stimuli, characteristic of each drive, separately conditioned, to which the animal would learn to make a different response. Hull believes that when a stimulus occurs in close conjunction with a response and this is followed by a reward (a reduction in drive) then this stimulus will be more likely to evoke the response on a future occasion. Now if an animal is made hungry and it turns left at a choice point in the maze and obtains a reward of food, then Hull supposes that it will be more likely to turn left when it is hungry again. The stimuli which occurred just before the animal turned will evoke the response which was followed by reward. These stimuli were the stimuli from the maze arising at the choice point (S_c) and the stimuli internal to the animal arising from hunger, which are called the drive stimuli of hunger (S_{Dh}). Thus S_{Dh} and S_c will jointly evoke R_L (the response of turning left). Therefore the animal when hungry will take the appropriate path. An analogous process occurs when the animal is rewarded by drinking for turning right when it is thirsty. The animal therefore learns to turn one way because the only sets of stimuli which are different when it is making a choice, the drive stimuli, have been differentially attached to the two responses. Kendler (1946), however, trained rats in a simple T-maze when they were simultaneously hungry and thirsty. There was water in one goal box and food in the other. All animals had equal opportunity to explore both goal boxes. In the test series the rats were made either hungry or thirsty, but not both. They were able to make the appropriate choice. This makes a difficulty for Hull. There was only a single pattern of drive stimuli during training, generated by the state of being simultaneously hungry and thirsty. The supposition that rats learn to respond differentially to diverse patterns of drive stimuli in making the choice is made unlikely.

[45]

The present hypothesis, on the other hand, presents another way of looking at this evidence. There are two links, one with analyzers (presumably in the mouth and stomach, as suggested above) which fire off when food is ingested, and the other when the water is ingested. These analyzers are attached to a primary link, which is excited by certain changes occurring around it. The one to which the "food" analyzer is innately attached is sensitive to changes occurring when there is a nutritional deficit, the other, to which the "drink" analyzer is attached, is excited when there is a water shortage. Now when either or both these links are excited, and the animal is thrown into activity, many analyzers attached to other links will be fired off in sequence and the links connected together in sequence. If, say, the already attached drink analyzer is fired off immediately after these, this sequence will be connected to the link to which the drink analyzer is attached and not the link to which the food analyzer is innately attached. Next time the link to which the innately connected drink analyzer is connected is excited indirectly by the appropriate chemical change, the row of links following it will also be excited. These will be the links whose analyzers fired off before the innately attached drink analyzer, whereas the link to which the food analyzer is fixed will not be attached to these links. Therefore, when the animal is thirsty, it will begin to look sequentially for those stimuli which occurred prior to its finding water. The same of course applies, *mutatis mutandis*, when it is hungry; the animal will again select that sequence which when it was "hungry" led to a "food" result, on account of the mechanism outlined. It clearly does not make a difference to this ability whether the animal was thirsty or not when it was hungry and found food (see also Deutsch, 1958).

In fairness to Hull it must be mentioned that following Spence's suggestion he attempted (1952) to explain this experiment in terms of the antedating goal response. But as will be shown later (chap. viii) this derivation is faulty.

Though the hypothesis advanced in the foregoing pages is capable of explaining the learning and performance of a single habit at a time, it must be expanded so that it may be applied to situations in which there is a choice. Let us, therefore, assume that there are many rows, with the properties described in a system all of which may control output. No further rule would need to be in-

[46]

corporated if all these were assumed to activate output in turn. But sometimes the system may be confronted with a choice.

13. The rule which is therefore added is that if there are two links competing by selecting incompatible output, the one with a higher rate of firing will secure output.

Now the rate of firing in an activated link is made to depend on the degree of activation of the link activating it and the threshold of the link being activated. One of the factors affecting the threshold is the temporary rise in threshold (the refractory period) in a link after the firing-off of the attached analyzer. Therefore, if an animal is trained equally on two habits of equal length and equal reward, and then allowed to choose between them on closely spaced successive trials, it will alternate regularly between them. This deduction is confirmed by the experimental work of Dennis (1939) and Heathers (1940).

Hull would, of course, predict the same (from the postulates concerning reactive inhibition). On the other hand, he would predict turn alternation, whereas the present theory in the usual situation demands what might be called stimulus, place, or goal alternation. The refractory period of a link is due to the firing-off of the attached analyzer. This leads to a temporary weakening of the "attractiveness" of those parts of the environment which have fired this analyzer. An experiment performed by Montgomery (1952) to test these alternative possibilities supports the deduction from the present hypothesis. This worker trained rats on an X-maze with equal reward on the two opposite ends of the straight arm of the X. He thus had a choice of starting point. If the animals alternate between turns, they should run toward the same goal if they are started from the two different starting points in succession. If they alternate on a principle of stimulus or goal alternation, they should alternate between the two goals in spite of executing two similar turning movements in a row. Montgomery found that the results obtained in this situation showed stimulus alternation. However, on the present hypothesis we should expect goal alternation. Montgomery's result could be predicted merely from a principle of stimulus alternation. Glanzer (1953) has suggested such an explanation of spontaneous alternation. He assumes that if a stimulus at the choice point has been effective in eliciting a response, its effectiveness will be diminished and only gradually return to normal. This supposition would explain Montgomery's result equally well.

[47]

However, such a theory would not explain goal alternation, which would be predicted in addition on the present hypothesis. Sutherland (1957) undertook to test this prediction—made in 1953—evidence on which was not available when the theory was first framed (Deutsch, 1953). If an animal is equally rewarded and trained on two sides of a T-maze where goal boxes are out of sight at the choice point, then if it is directly placed in one of the two goal boxes and rewarded there, it should tend to run to the other when it is placed again at the entrance of the maze and given a free choice. It appears from Sutherland's experiment that such is in fact the case. This tends to confirm the notion, unique to the theory, that "motivational" excitation is transmitted through units underlying acts nearer the goal to those farther away from it and that stimulation far from increasing this excitation actually severs its flow.

V

Curiosity and Exploration

It has often been suggested (e.g., Montgomery, 1952) that spontaneous alternation is due to exploration or curiosity. It has been shown by many (Berlyne, Dember) that rats will approach novel stimuli. If a rat has just turned one way in the alternation situation, then it is likely that it will turn the other, because this is the way which is more novel. However, such a suggestion seems unlikely. Sutherland (1957) has found that rats will alternate and run to the other goal box after they have been placed in one goal box. Berlyne and Slater (1957) in an excellent study have found that rats will not learn to run to a goal box in a T-maze where they are presented with novel stimuli, even though they explore these when they come across them in the goal box. It appears that a rat will not choose a path merely because there is a novel stimulus at the end of it which it cannot see. In Sutherland's experiment, both maze arms in the T-maze were equally novel. It was only one of the goal boxes, which the animal could not see, which was less recent or more novel and it sought this box out. If the box which it ran to was more novel, it could not have been chosen on the basis of its novelty because Berlyne and Slater have shown that animals do not choose a goal box even when it contains stimuli far more novel than those to be found in a goal box that has been very frequently visited and found to be, time after time, monotonously the same by the rat. It is, therefore, not the case that spontaneous alternation can be accounted for in terms of curiosity or exploration.

This is not to deny that "curiosity" can be the cause of alternation in cases where the situation is unfamiliar to the animal (Kivy *et al.*, Dember). This leads us to the problem of curiosity. Curiosity has been assumed by many (e.g., Berlyne, 1950) to be a drive, like hunger or thirst, with novel stimuli playing the part of food or

[49]

water. A novel stimulus will cause approach in a rat (and to that extent we may call it drive-producing, if we like this way of talking). This has been shown by Berlyne (1950, 1955) and Thompson and Solomon (1954), among others. These authors have also found that "novelty" wears off quickly. Berlyne (1955) states that a permanent decrement in exploration of a novel object occurs after the first minute. Montgomery (1953) found that a decrement in exploratory behavior generalizes to similar situations and that this decrement decreases in magnitude as the similarity of the stimulus situation decreases. Montgomery (1951) has also shown what might have been predicted from the above observations, that rats tended to traverse that part of the maze occupied least recently and so to explore it in an orderly and systematic manner.

So far the evidence shows that animals do attempt to maximize the stimulation from cues which are unfamiliar, and we might, therefore, conclude that exploration is indeed like hunger or thirst. But this would cause a difficulty for the theory as it has been stated so far. We should have to imagine some pool of "novel" analyzers all connected to a primary link which they would also excite in the manner of the internal medium. From this pool would have to be detached all those analyzers which had already been stimulated for a certain period. Other links would also be attached to this primary link when one of the novel analyzers fired off, to subserve a learning function. This does not sound in the least plausible. We have to inquire in what other ways exploration or curiosity resembles a drive. When a hungry rat after a sequence of stimuli finds food, it will seek out these stimuli again. Will a rat similarly learn a maze merely for the sake of seeing a novel object? Montgomery (1954) believes that they do. He attached a Dashiell maze, which is a large square with a large number of intersecting paths to one side of a Y-maze. His rats came to choose this side, and later, when he reversed the position of the Dashiell maze by putting it on the other arm of the Y, the rats also reversed their choice. However, the factor of novelty in the Dashiell maze is confounded with that of spaciousness. The rats may have been reacting to this situation in terms of their escape tendencies.

Berlyne and Slater (1957) in a study already quoted, by controlling for the factors of spaciousness and complexity found that novelty per se was not rewarding to rats. They trained rats in a Y-maze where one arm always led to a novel card and the other to a familiar card. In spite of the fact that novel stimuli were recognized as such if we take exploration as a criterion, the animals failed to show any tendency to choose the side which contained the novel stimuli. The animals approached and explored the novel cards more than the familiar (the probability of the difference being significant at the .001 level), but in spite of this their novelty was not rewarding.

Berlyne and Slater also performed their experiment with two other groups of rats under the same conditions, except that for one group the reward was not a novel object but simply a large goal box as opposed to a blind, and for the other a goal box containing a variety of objects as opposed to an empty goal box. These groups found spaciousness and complexity rewarding. Similar factors may be operating in monkeys in whom curiosity has also been postulated as a drive. It seems, therefore, that this important experiment shows that exploration is not a drive like hunger or thirst. The consequences of its satisfaction are not rewarding.

It is possible to accommodate the somewhat paradoxical properties of novel stimuli in the present framework if we make one assumption. This is that a secondary link, before it becomes attached to other links, generates some spontaneous activity. Then, as its analyzer is stimulated, it will, according to rule 5 "be switched to control the motor system and the link will act to maximize its own stimulation." In this way an animal will approach and explore a novel stimulus object, as has been shown to be the case in the experiments quoted above. Why does this exploration cease? It will cease according to rule 9, which states that links have their excitability diminished when they become connected to other stimuli when these occur together, through inhibitory connections (according to 9). This is because a group of novel stimuli will become connected together via their links or will become connected to stimuli already connected up. In this way it can be seen that novel stimuli should be attractive though not rewarding. Having become connected together, and to other links, the previously novel links will not have so much excitation to switch into the motor system when their analyzers are again stimulated, unless they derive it from a primary link. If their analyzers are not stimulated (if the previously novel object is not present to the animal), they will not produce enough excitation to transmit through other links to alter an animal's choice, as old stimuli on the other side of the choice will be producing a simi-

[51]

lar amount. For before the novel links were connected together, their activity summed in producing an approach response. When they are connected together, the activity of each will be divided. An alternative suggestion which has points of greater plausibility is that it is not only links which have been previously unconnected which fire, but that it is the actual process of any link being connected which makes it fire. In this way novel combinations of non-novel cues would provoke approach and not totally novel stimuli. (I owe this suggestion to my wife.)

On the above suppositions we should expect animals with more unconnected links to indulge in a greater amount of exploratory activity. Such animals would either be young animals or animals whose experience has been artificially restricted. Such is the finding of Thompson and Heron (1954). These workers studied the effects of restricting the early experience of dogs on their subsequent exploratory activity. They found that animals with a sensorily monotonous environment explore more than normal animals and that younger dogs explore more than older dogs. They also found that exploratory activity declines with the time of exposure to a situation. This is in agreement with the theory.

These suggestions concerning the phenomena called curiosity in the rat are only tentative. Explanations in terms of curiosity of a whole range of probably heterogeneous phenomena have become popular. For instance, an animal's exploration, when allegedly all its basic drives are satisfied, is held to be a manifestation of curiosity or exploratory drive. Unfortunately the animal's basic drives are only incompletely known. It does not appear to be known that the laboratory rat has a very strong drive to construct burrows. Being interested in the nest-building behavior of domestic rabbits which had been kept in hutches all their lives and finding patterns of great complexity (Deutsch, 1957), the writer placed laboratory rats in a tank with a large quantity of earth. The creatures, in spite of no previous contact with earth, turned out to be indefatigable burrowers. Subsequent observations showed that a single rat when placed in the tank filled with earth would start to dig, often within 5 minutes, and that it would dig a tunnel measuring many feet within the first 24 hours. The entrance to the tunnel would tend to be under a projection. (That is why the earth was given a steep slope at one side of the tank. Otherwise the rat would dig against the side of the tank and stop, as it could only go vertically downward.) The animal would also place the burrow entrance in the darkest portion of the tank. The rat when digging would display a variety of actions as striking and specialized as those displayed in mating. The concentration, excitement, and single-mindedness (if we may be anthropomorphic) of a burrowing rat would seem, prima facie, to betoken the presence of a strong drive, and one of which psychology is ignorant. Perhaps there are other drives similarly unfulfilled, such as the acquisition of a territory, motivating the cage-bred rat when we see it exploring. We simply do not know the rat well enough as an animal to invoke such entities as a curiosity drive with any certainty on most of the occasions where it has allegedly been observed. Berlyne and Slater have indeed made a start in separating such things as novelty from spaciousness and complexity. But it is unlikely that a rat prefers places just because they are complex or spacious. What has to be determined is what precise stimulus combinations evoke this preference. What these factors are is most likely to emerge from studies with these animals in semifree environments.

VI

Reward and Reinforcement

The factor leading to reinforcement has already been mentioned in passing in the last chapter. It is necessary to expand and defend this statement as the topic of reward is a controversial one in present-day psychology. The view adopted is a natural extension of that of the role of stimulation adopted in explaining need. It is argued that there is no difference in the mechanism of primary and secondary reinforcement and that the factor leading to reinforcement (to use the usual language) is the firing-off of an analyzer already attached to a link which can receive motivational excitation. This firing will lead to the connection to this link of other links so that they in turn receive motivational excitation. (Motivational excitation is excitation derived directly or indirectly from a primary link.)

An examination of experimental evidence by Sheffield will elucidate the hypothesis to the reader and will, it is hoped, provide a convincing explanation of it. Sheffield and co-workers (Sheffield and Roby, 1950; Wulff and Backer, 1951) have found that copulation without ejaculation is a primary reinforcing factor in rats or, to put it in another way, possesses reward value which does not diminish with time. They have also found that the taste of saccharin, though non-nutritive, appears to have primary reinforcing properties. These findings constitute a puzzle for those who say that tension reduction or biological need reduction leads to reinforcement. On the present hypothesis the findings form no exception and could have been predicted. As the rat has an unlearned preference for saccharin and aims at copulation without previous accidental experience of it, it is inferred that the analyzers signaling a sweet taste (or the various stages of copulation) are connected permanently and innately to the first part of a row of links, the first one or few being primary. This being the case, any links whose analyzers fired off previously to

[54]

these will be connected to the end of that row of links. Next time the row of links is activated, the previously unattached part will be activated too, with the consequence that an animal will now seek out not only the stimulation (or stimulus-configuration) innately attractive to it, but also that stimulation which occurred previously to this stimulation on a past occasion. Thus learning will have taken place in the same manner as it is always supposed to occur on the present hypothesis.

It should be mentioned that the results of the experiments by Sheffield and his co-workers have not gone unquestioned. Smith and Capretta (1956) have performed an experiment in which they show that the reward value of saccharin diminishes if animals are allowed to drink it only when they are hungry and when the processes of digestion are presumably complete. They point out that in previous experiments saccharin was administered when primary need reduction in the form of nutriment absorbed from the gut could have been occurring while the animal was receiving the taste of saccharin. A group of their own rats was given a saccharin solution to drink not long after they had fed, and for this group saccharin kept its reward value. Hence Smith and Capretta argue that animals learn to like saccharin through primary reinforcement. However, this experiment is inconclusive. Large quantities of saccharin solution on an empty stomach may have their unpleasant effects. It would be more satisfactory to perform the experiment on animals with esophageal fistulas. In this way any possible untoward aftereffects of excessive fluid intake would be avoided. It seems unlikely that the taste for saccharin is due to secondary reinforcement because of the finding of De Snoo, that foetuses *in utero* would respond by drinking amniotic fluid when saccharin had been introduced into it. This is before they had eaten at all, of course. This is why Smith and Capretta's findings cannot be taken at their face value. Kagan (1955) has compared further the reward value of incomplete and complete sexual behavior. He finds that rats not allowed to ejaculate after a time develop some kind of conflict in this situation, approaching the female and yet being reluctant to mount her. Here it is possible that uncompleted coition may produce a severe discomfort. It seems then that the evidence of Sheffield and co-workers can still be interpreted in the way it has been above.

Further evidence that reward is a function of the afferent message has been obtained by Deutsch and Jones (1959) in an experi-

[55]

ment quoted above (p. 31). It appears that hypotonic saline generates less of a "water" signal in the rat's gustatory apparatus. As a consequence a rat will ingest a much larger quantity of this fluid than of ordinary water when both are available ad libitum, as would be predicted by the present theory. However, as a corollary of this when the animal is given the choice between fixed and equal amounts of water and saline, it will learn to choose the water. This can be explained if we assume that it is the afferent message generated by the reward substance which is the factor responsible for reward.

There are some other predictions from the hypothesis which should be discussed.

The firing of two analyzers in sequence is on the present hypothesis responsible for the connection of their two links. This connection enables excitation originating from a primary link to pass from one of these links to the other, if one of them is already so connected as to receive this excitation when it arises. However, it is this firing-off in succession of two analyzers which is a prerequisite of such a connection and so of what may eventually be demonstrated by the system as learning.

Thus it is predicted that if an animal is placed in a maze hungry and its physiological deficiency is artificially corrected in the goal box, this need reduction will not act as "reward." For what leads to learning is the touching-off of analyzers. Thus the taste of saccharin acts as a reward, whereas glucose, untasted and unfelt in the stomach, it is predicted will not. Similarly, an abolition of thirst by the injection of water will not be rewarding.

There are, however, some recent experiments which appear to contradict this view. The first is by Coppock and Chambers (1954), who actually performed the experiment of rewarding an animal with glucose injected directly into the blood stream and found that this had a reinforcing effect. A more detailed examination of their experiment will show its more precise relevance to the main contention of the present theory. The experimenters used thirty-two male albino rats with animals ranging from 240 to 360 gm. in weight. These they deprived of food for 3 days (72 hours), apparently without accustoming them to any schedule previously. The animals would thus be almost moribund. They inserted the rats into a snugly fitting cage, with head and neck protruding. When the rat's head deviated from the midline, it interrupted an infrared beam, which in turn operated a relay. Sixteen of the rats inserted into this apparatus had an intravenous injection of 10 per cent glucose in physiological saline. The other rats received only saline.

The authors claim that the rats learned to turn their heads to the side on which the relay turned on the glucose injection. However, they admit that significant differences were not obtained for absolute frequency of head turns or their absolute duration or for the relative number of moves toward a position, but only for the relative duration of preference for the rewarded position. They also admit that their controls were inadequate. "Additional controls would be necessary to evaluate satiation, revival, response generalisation and other factors contributing to total activity." The controls they used were in fact inappropriate. Differences in behavior uncorrelated with any reward factors may be due to physiological differences between animals given a nutritious solution after three days' starvation and those left in a depleted state. It would have been more satisfactory if the authors had given glucose to both groups, with the control group receiving the injection at random intervals in the quantities earned by the experimental group.

However, even if the experimental result is accepted, we may infer from the extraordinarily long period of food deprivation imposed on the animals that the experimenters could not obtain any result at shorter intervals. This means that the mechanism of reward operating in this instance was different from that in ordinary eating where there is no marked depletion when reinforcement occurs. The present hypothesis does not deny that alleviation of pain or severe discomfort can act as reinforcement. It asserts merely that this is not the mechanism in appetitive behavior before extreme depletion develops. Some further experiments by Chambers (1956a, 1956b) are also relevant. In a further study on dogs and rabbits he attempted to repeat the experiments previously performed on rats. The animals in this experiment were placed in a cylindrical activity box and were allowed to move around in this apparatus. They were given a glucose injection when they were in a certain area of the box and saline or xylose (a nonnutritive sugar) when they were in other positions. The dogs were either not starved at all or starved for 1 or 3 days. They failed to show any evidence of learning. Chambers says: "The fact that dogs were not available for longer periods of starvation should be considered."

[57]

A similar experiment on 6-, 4-, and 3-day-starved rabbits was successful. The level of depletion of these animals, unaccustomed to any schedule, must have been extreme. An injection of glucose could have had consequences in terms of revival which are normally absent when an animal finds food rewarding. Chambers himself suspected that some factor of revival might have been operating and checked this in a further experiment. In this he found that 4-day-starved rabbits did respond in a way which might account for the rewarding effect of the glucose injections.

> Within relatively short periods of time after injections, the glucose injections were followed by significant rises in body temperature at some surface areas and slight changes in breathing rates. These results may possibly account for some of the rewarding properties of nutritive injections. . . . The animals may have experienced a general feeling of body warmth, and this may have been rewarding to the food-deprived animals.

There were probably many such factors stemming from a rapid amelioration in the condition of the animals which must have been severely ill from starvation. But these effects are more difficult to measure; these findings leave us free to think (or perhaps make us more convinced than before) that such is not the normal mechanism of food reward.

Another experiment which constitutes prima facie evidence against the theory has been reported by Thomson and Porter (1953). These experimenters rendered six rats ageusic and anosmic. These, along with eight normal rats, were fed on a sodium-deficient diet. All these rats were trained in a T-maze in which saline, subthreshold for the operated rats, was placed on one side and distilled water on the other. Five non-deficient normal rats were also trained. Four trials a day were given, about 15 minutes apart. The ageusic as well as the normal non-deficient group did not learn after 10 days. The deficient normal group did. So far the findings support the present theory against those which regard primary need reduction as both sufficient and necessary for reinforcement. However, at this point the experimenters adopted a special training procedure arranged in a series of steps.

1. They gave the ageusic animals, who were under 12 hours of water deprivation, 4 days of alternating free and forced runs, the forced trials to the side not chosen in the free trials.

[58]

2. The rats were then given four trials per day for 2 days on which all the choices were free. On these days the rats were not water deprived.

3. Then followed 2 days without water deprivation on which all trials were forced to the correct side.

4. To establish whether the animals had learned, they were allowed a free choice without water deprivation for 3 days, again with four trials a day. However, only four rats out of six appear to have learned.

5. For two rats (out of six) still choosing the saline at a 50 per cent level only, steps 1 and 4 were repeated with the saline solution raised to superthreshold strength (0.8 per cent). These two rats "promptly came to choose correctly during step 5," that is, they learned immediately they were able to taste the salt.

6. Lastly, for the four rats not in step 5 and four deprived normals, extinction trials were run with distilled water in both goal boxes. Extinction took place, thus showing that learning of the position of the saline had taken place and that the behavior observed was not a mere artifact due to the development of a side preference.

In this stage of the experiment it was demonstrated, if we accept the result granted of the limitations of the experiment, that need reduction can have a reinforcing function. Again the result here is presumably to be ascribed to a long-term alleviation of discomfort under severe conditions of deficiency. On the other hand, the experiment makes it improbable that the salty taste becomes rewarding by secondary reinforcement in the normal animal but rather that it is innately rewarding. The ageusic animals would be in the same situation on the secondary reinforcement view as young animals which have to learn that a salty taste is associated with primary need reduction. However, these ageusic animals could not learn to associate other stimuli with this type of need reduction in the ordinary learning situation. Only a specially designed training schedule enabled the animals to learn the connection—and even then some animals failed. Such an elaborate and favorable situation for learning hardly existed in the animals' previous experience, and yet even the two recalcitrant rats learned promptly as soon as they could taste the salt (as did the deficient controls). These recalcitrants must have been poor learners. If the special training did not effect learning in them, it is hardly plausible to believe that they could have learned on the proposed mechanism in their usual cage environment. It is difficult to see how a rat kept under the usual laboratory conditions can learn that a particular deficiency is corrected by ingesting a substance having a particular taste. A rat is usually fed all its life on a composite food, which stimulates, whenever it is eaten, the same, or a highly similar, population of taste receptors. The animal has all its deficiencies corrected at once and the correcting of a particular deficiency is always accompanied by a stimulation of all the taste receptors which are always stimulated when the animal eats. It, therefore, has no possibility of correlating a particular taste with the diminution of a particular need or discomfort. How a specific taste could therefore be ascribed correctly to a particular alleviation of discomfort is left a mystery.

The view that an appetite for salt when deficiency arises appears without learning is supported by the experiment of Epstein and Stellar. These workers adrenalectomized two groups of rats. One group, consisting of four rats, was allowed immediate postoperative access to a 3 per cent salt solution and tap water in a two-bottle preference situation. The second group consisted of twelve rats. These were deprived of salt until they reached a certain criterion of deficiency measured by water intake and fall in body weight. This criterion was so strict that six animals died before reaching it. The first group gradually increased their salt intake. The second group consumed large amounts of salt immediately upon being allowed access to it. These workers conclude:

> Post-operative experience with salt solutions is not a necessary condition for the development of the exaggerated specific hunger for salt in the adrenalectomised rat. The gradually increasing preference for salt exhibited post-operatively by these animals (Group I) represents primarily their response to a gradually increasing physiological need for the sodium ion. When that need is allowed to develop in the absence of experience (Group II), salt intake reaches the exaggerated post-operative levels immediately.

Epstein and Stellar in a subsidiary experiment upset artificially the relation between the amount of salt ingested and its need-reducing effects. They fed to the animals ion-exchange resins, which absorbed about one-half of the ingested concentration of the sodium ion, this being replaced by potassium and ammonium ions. This exchange occurs in the upper digestive tract before the ingested saline is absorbed. (It is a procedure which in many ways resembles the use of an esophageal fistula for the purpose of preventing the entry of water or food into the digestive system, as in the experiments of Hull or Bellows. It is similarly used to test the behavior or the system involved when the relation of ingestion or motor activity to need satisfaction is altered.) When the animals have been fed on this ion-exchange resin, their salt intake goes up sharply after the first trial. On the first trial after treatment the ion-exchange resin would not have had any effect, as it acts on the saline which is ingested after the resin has been administered. The sharp increase on the record trial takes place even though the relation between any previous salt need and experience with the taste of salt is now quite altered. We can, of course, believe that the effects of all previous learning are altered without trial and error on the strength of a single trial, but this seems somewhat implausible.

Such results are, on the other hand, quite in accordance with the view put forward here. A primary link sensitive to a salt deficit and connected to salt receptors would give the behavior which has been observed. As soon as there arose a salt deficit, this would irritate the primary link sensitive to this change. The animal would ingest salt which in turn would stimulate certain taste receptors. These receptors, connected to the irritated primary link, would discharge. The impinging of this discharge on the primary link would in turn lessen the sensitivity of the primary link to the condition caused by the salt deficiency. The animal would thus ingest a quantity of salt solution proportionate to the stimulation of the salt receptors by this salt solution which was occurring and the extent of the irritation of the primary link. If the relation between the amount tasted and the alleviation of deficiency is altered so that the animal tastes too much in relation to the amount of alleviation of deficiency, there should be no change on the first trial but the animal should drink the same amount more frequently. This is because the amount tasted and so ingested will be insufficient to relieve the internal demand which will therefore, being higher, begin to irritate the primary link sooner. If, as in Epstein and Stellar's experiment, the animal is not given an opportunity of drinking more frequently, the internal demand will rise much further than usual and irritate the primary link to a greater extent than in the normal case. Hence the quantity consumed on the second trial will rise abruptly, a greater amount of receptor discharge being necessary to neutralize the excitatory effects of the enhanced deficit. On the other hand, it is predicted, if the relation of the receptor discharge to the alleviation of deficiency is altered in the other direction so that the animal, though it tastes less, consumes a greater amount of the substance of which it is in need, the amount of the deficient substance ingested on the first trial ought to be much larger than normal and decrease steeply on subsequent trials, provided these are widely spaced. If the animal is allowed continuous access to the needed substance, it ought first of all to consume a supernormal amount. After this there ought to be a long period during which no more is consumed. This would be predicted because on the first trial a given amount of the needed substance would not cause the usual amount of excitation in the receptors responsible for signaling its ingestion. Therefore, the amount of discharge impinging on the primary link initiating the activity of ingestion would be smaller than usual per unit of substance ingested. (Hence, more substance would be ingested than normal before the irritability of the primary link was reduced below threshold.) Once ingested, the substance would be absorbed, and, provided the excess was not excreted or stored, an abnormally large time should elapse before the deficit should make itself felt again. However, when the animal starts drinking or eating again, it should continue again for a longer time. Similar predictions can be made concerning hunger and thirst.

The other consequence of this hypothesis concerns the rewarding effects of the salty taste. The discharge of a receptor system, whether innately or otherwise, is postulated to be responsible for "reinforcement." In the first part of Thomson and Porter's experiment the normal salt-deficient rats would connect the sequence of links, the firing of whose analyzers had preceded the discharge of the "salt" analyzer, to the row of links which was excited by the primary link to which this salt analyzer was connected. Hence, salt deprivation would throw all the links to which they were connected into activity. According to the system described in the previous chapter, the animal would make its way to the place where the salt taste had been registered. When this happens, learning is said to have occurred. On the other hand, if the animal is rendered ageusic, the salt receptors cannot be stimulated and therefore cannot lead to any sort of "registration" or reinforcement. No links are attached to the primary salt link as the salt analyzer has never fired. However, should the threshold of this analyzer be exceeded, learning should be prompt. The hypothesis thus shows good agreement with the evidence and makes a testable prediction.

It will be said that the present theory has in fact to postulate two factors to explain the evidence concerning reward. This is true if we include cases of deprivation so great as to cause physical suffering. If we take the more usual case where an animal eats or drinks without undue depletion, the stimulus-arrival theory can be used to account for an overwhelming portion of the phenomena while the stimulus-reduction theory of primary reinforcement does not appear even to describe the residual factors. This is made clear by the work of Sheffield, Roby, and Campbell (1954). In the first portion of their experiment they took four groups of rats each and placed them on a diet of 8 gm. of mash per day. They trained these on a runway with, alternately: tap water, a solution of saccharin, a solution of dextrose, and a mixture of the saccharin and dextrose solution. They found saccharin to be reinforcing. Dextrose was only reinforcing when saccharin was added. The mixture of saccharin and dextrose was the most reinforcing. The authors say that this mixture tasted sweetest to the human observer. To rule out the possibility that the dextrose was not rewarding because the animals had not had sufficient experience of the nutritive properties of dextrose, other groups of rats were put on the same feeding schedule as those in the first part of the experiment. They were then given experience in a replica of the goal box with either water or dextrose. The animals with consummatory responses previously reinforced by nourishment did no better than controls when trained to run toward dextrose as in the first experiment. This does not agree with Hull's third postulate, which states: "Whenever an effector activity (R) is closely associated with a stimulus efferent impulse or trace (S) and the conjunction is closely associated with the rapid diminution in the motivational stimulus (S_D or S_G) there will result an increment (Δ) to a tendency for that stimulus to evoke that response" (1952, p. 6). However, this evidence does support the notion that a certain type of stimulation per se acts as reward.

It might be objected that in Sheffield, Roby, and Campbell's experiment the dextrose was never ingested in sufficient quantities in the learning situation to have a rewarding effect. The animals appear to have drunk very little dextrose. However, the experiment

[63]

still shows that the taste of dextrose was not learned as being rewarding. It does show that saccharin, in spite of not being need-reducing, was rewarding.

The taste of saccharin is regarded on the present theory as rewarding because the analyzer relaying it is held to be innately attached to the mechanism of hunger. It is assumed that eating is turned off mainly by messages coming from the stomach but that there are some gustatory messages concerned. Now saccharin generates gustatory messages alone without affecting the stomach in the way ordinary food substances do. As a result, ingestion of this substance should be excessive, as it will not be as effective in turning off ingestive activity and its rewarding effects should be less powerful than those of a substance which has the same taste but which exerts an effect via the stomach. On this view an animal ingesting saccharin is very like the animal ingesting a nutritious substance when it is hyperphagic owing to the absence of the ventromedial nucleus of the hypothalamus. It has been posited that the ventromedial nucleus relays the message from the stomach of the animal and that this message has an inhibitory effect on further eating. Now in the saccharin-ingesting animal no message from the stomach is generated: in the case of the hyperphagic, such a message is not passed on or relayed. In neither case does the message arrive. Therefore, when ingesting saccharin, the hyperphagic animal and the normal animal should behave in the same way. However, there are probable complications in the case of saccharin. Excessive quantities of saccharin may begin to taste bitter. Saccharin in high concentrations tastes bitter. It also causes a bitter taste when it is injected, whereas glucose tastes sweet. Large amounts of saccharin solution when they are ingested may cause too large a concentration of saccharin in the blood stream with similar effects. Some other sweet-tasting substance might be preferable from an experimental point of view.

There is other suggestive evidence to show that it is the afferent message which is the important factor in reinforcement. Guttman (1954) has found those solutions of glucose and sucrose which are judged to be equally sweet by human observers are also equally reinforcing to rats. Hutt (1954) has found that the rate of responding (during periodic reinforcement) of rats in a Skinner box is a function of both the taste and the amount of reward.

ELECTRICAL SELF-STIMULATION
OF THE BRAIN

No discussion of reward and reinforcement would today be complete without a reference to the interesting work of Olds (1958) on the rewarding effects of direct brain stimulation. Olds has found that rats will learn to press levers or run mazes in order to obtain electric stimulation of certain parts of the midbrain and hypothalamus. Though there are local variations, the rate of lever-pressing to obtain this stimulation is very high (rates of 7,000 per hour are reported) and the "appetite" for the stimulation does not in general undergo satiation. In spite of these high rates of responding maintained for a long time and the appearance of a high reward value, extinction occurs very quickly. If the animal finds that pressing the lever produces no more stimulation, it seems promptly to lose interest. There are, therefore, at least two atypical features in this behavior. First, most intensely rewarding activity shows satiation, and, second, most intensely rewarding activity is slow to extinguish. Otherwise this kind of learning seems much like the normal. It demonstrates neatly one of the contentions of the present work that it is the arrival of stimulation which is rewarding. (Olds also shows that a separate system is concerned with avoidance, again one of the contentions of the writer.) There need be nothing mysterious about electrical stimulation being rewarding. If a reward is due to the arrival of a message in the brain, then it should be possible to "deceive" the brain by inserting the message in it through electrical stimulation. For instance, if the ventromedial nucleus of the hypothalamus plays the part of the analyzer to the "hunger" unit in the present theory, it should be possible, by stimulating it electrically, to make it pass a message to the primary link. This it usually does only when food arrives in the stomach. Hence, first, the system will behave as if food had arrived in the stomach and the animal will tend to stop eating, and, second, any link whose analyzer fired off before the message will be fastened to the primary link, because the primary link sends out a message which has this effect. It has been found by Smith (1956) that electrical stimulation of the ventromedial hypothalamus does decrease eating, but it is not known whether it has an effect equivalent specifically to a food reward, as is predicted by the present theory.

But it is clear that the reward effect found by Olds cannot be due to a stimulation of the analyzers attached to primary links. We should expect that, if it were, there would be a pronounced tendency to satiation, the animal would work to obtain the stimulation only when appropriately motivated, and extinction curves should be normal. It would be interesting to test this prediction, for instance, in the case of the ventromedial nucleus.

What part of the system described by the present theory could Olds have been stimulating? At a guess it appears that his electrodes were exciting mainly the paths which usually carry excitation to other links when the primary links are excited. To support this hypothesis, there is the fact that food intake, for instance, was increased owing to stimulation which had this rewarding effect. Such a supposition would also account for the apparently high "drive" level of the animal to secure this type of stimulation and its insatiability. The animal should persist in responding at a high rate because, with each electrical stimulus, excitation occurs along the pathways which carry it to other links and to the motor system. This excitation normally originates in the intact animal in the primary links and is due to their biochemical irritation. When this biochemical irritation ceases, so will the excitation and the animal will no longer be inclined to act. We might, if our guess is correct, expect something of a similar nature to happen with the animals which are being artificially excited. If we suppose that the cells excited electrically do not persist in their excitement long after the stimulation has been withdrawn, then extinction ought to seem unusually swift, and this has been found. The hypothesis is that "extinction" appears quickly because of the swift disappearance of motivational excitation. The results of Sidman *et al.* (1955) support this interpretation. They found that low ratios of rewarded to non-rewarded trials and brief intervals were necessary to maintain partial reinforcement lever-pressing in the electrical stimulation situation. In effect, the electrical stimulus from the last press provides "motivation" for the next, but this "motivation" dissipates quickly with time. This suggestion could be tested by recording activity through the stimulating electrodes before and after stimulation. If we measure before stimulation, we should obtain the basal rate of excitation in the tissue to be excited. If we measure after the cessation of stimulation, leaving a short time for any artifact to disappear, we should then measure the enhancement of excitation due to the electrical stimulation and correlate its decay with extinction curves obtained with the electrode in this position.

So far the persistence and insatiability of the behavior have been accounted for, together with its unusually rapid tendency to extinction. We have not, however, explained the rewarding nature of the stimulation. On the present hypothesis an enhancement of excitation from anything but the analyzer does not serve a rewarding function. It is to be remembered, however, that when one link receives a message that its analyzer has been fired, this has the effect either of lowering the threshold for the passage of excitation between itself and another link, the analyzer of which has just fired, or of connecting it with this link. This effect can be achieved only if there is some kind of signal or message sent from one link to another, equivalent to saying, "Connect," or "Reduce resistance." On the present view the implanted electrode causes messages to run down this channel too, because this is a pathway which would have to run very close, at least in parts, to the channel conveying "motivational" excitation.

This suggestion is again independently verifiable. With more refined electrode techniques, we should be able to separate out the "reward" effect from the excitatory effect. It should be possible, for instance, to cause an animal, only when it is itself hungry, to repeat an action by rewarding it by stimulation in a locus which neither increased its appetite nor diminished it. Further we should be able to "excite" it by selective means and obtain enhanced activity without this being rewarding to the animal. For instance, using Andersson's technique of placing substances in the hypothalamus, we should find that excitation of a primary link does not prove rewarding per se. We would not expect a hypertonic solution which excites the animal in a more physiological manner to prove rewarding, as the tract carrying messages about "reinforcement" would not also be stimulated. It is already a prediction from the theory that the injection of a hypotonic solution which relieves thirst would not prove rewarding either.

Figure 6 illustrates the system undergoing externally imposed electrical stimulation. Two parallel pathways connect the links. The excitation of one pathway (b) leads the system to seek out any cue which stimulates an analyzer attached to an excited link. The excitation of the other pathway (a) leads the system to connect any link whose analyzer has fired to the link down whose pathway this

[67]

excitation has occurred. If the two links are already connected, excitation down this pathway (*a*) leads to a diminished "resistance" to the passage of excitation between these two links in pathway *b*. Hence excitation produced by electrode *a* stimulating these two pathways will lead to the seeking-out of the cues which occurred before such electrical stimulation and the persistence of such an attraction only while the excitation provoked in pathway *b* persists (unless this excitation is actually naturally provided by the excitation in the primary link due to the internal medium).

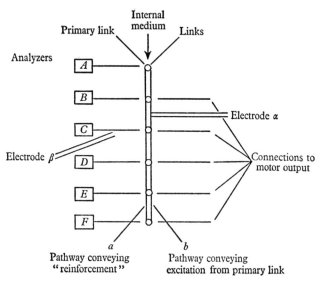

FIG. 6.—A diagram of the system, as used by Olds (1958), undergoing externally imposed electrical stimulation.

Stimulation by electrode *β* should produce a different effect, depending on the connections which it is stimulating most. If it is stimulating the connection from the analyzer alone, it should have no direct behavioral effect, as it is merely stopping transmission through link *C* and giving false information about the amount of stimulation from a cue which the animal is not actually attempting to maximize, as there is no excitation down the row of links. However, it should lead to the connecting to the link *C* of link *D*, whose analyzer is stimulated when the animal presses the lever. Therefore, on a subsequent occasion when excitation does flow down the row of links and the animal is in the box, the animal should have a tendency to press the lever without any electrical stimulation, but only a few times.

If electrode β is also stimulating link C and the pathways leading from it, the animal should attempt to approximate itself to the hallucinatory cue which would normally excite the pathway from analyzer C, while at the same time approximating itself to the cue stimulating analyzer D, which will be stimulated by lever-pressing. This conflict should slow down the rate of responding.

ii

IMPRINTING

Imprinting is a form of learning which is in many ways *sui generis* and which cannot be made to fit the same descriptive statements or generalizations as other types of learning. An excellent summary of the work on imprinting is given by Thorpe (1956, pp. 115–18). It appears that some birds, most notably geese, will adopt any moving object they see for a brief period after hatching and treat it as they would a parent.

Even if we disregard the fact that such learning occurs only during the earliest period of the animal's life and that it is of a remarkably permanent nature, there are still features about it which render it distinctive and unique. It is learning which occurs without any apparent reward. This feature of learning without a reward is not unique by itself. Latent learning, or learning without any obvious reward, can be quoted. However, the case of imprinting is different. Here we have the learning of a reward, not merely the learning of a what-leads-to-what. The stimuli imprinted are not a secondary reward because their attractiveness is apparently stable without other further reinforcement, and because they were first acquired seemingly without any reinforcement. Usually stimuli which have been latent-learned become attractive only when they become subgoals, the attainment of which enables the animal to reach some primary goal. For instance, the animal must be made hungry before it will run the maze (which it has learned when it was not hungry) in order to reach the goal of food. However, in the case of imprinting, it is different. The animal learns a primary goal or reward, for the stimuli which impinge on it for a certain time for a brief period during its existence become rewarding in themselves, like food or water. This is quite exceptional and unlike any other example of learning

[69]

familiar to experimental psychologists (except perhaps the speech of parrots and the learning of songs by songbirds [Thorpe, 1956]). Such a phenomenon would also not be predicted by the present theory. On the present theory a stimulus can be a goal when it is attached to an excited link. Such an attachment is due to one of two different factors. Either it can be determined through the mechanism of natural selection in such a way that the animal has at birth certain analyzers fixed to certain links, called "primary." We presume that this is the case with hunger and thirst and drives of a similar sort. Such attachments determine the primary goals of the organism. Or, alternatively, excitation can reach the link when analyzers already attached to other links which motivational excitation can reach fire off. In this way subgoals are formed which are sought out when the animal strives to reach the primary goals. If these subgoals fail to lead to the primary goals, they fail eventually to be sought out themselves.

Now, in the case of imprinting, it looks as if analyzers become connected to a primary link through experience in the way that other analyzers signaling food or water are fixed innately. It is as if what the animal regarded as food was determined by what it tasted first. This would of course be a possibility, but it would only be compatible with species survival if the odds were overwhelmingly in favor of the first thing tasted also forming a beneficial and adequate diet. Even then it is unlikely that natural selection would favor animals which have to learn—and this for the following reasons. A learning system is by its very nature an uneconomical system because of the number of elements it has to employ and the number of elements which are left unused when learning is completed. A mechanism of learning selects from a number of alternatives. It has this in common with an automatic telephone exchange. It would be folly to connect a telephone via the exchange if all that was ever to be required was always one and the same subscriber. The automatic exchange enables us to select any subscriber out of a great many. Having selected him, the mechanism for selection becomes redundant. Therefore, if we can forecast in advance what connection we shall need, it is better to dispense with the mechanism of selection altogether and simply to connect both subscribers together when we build the system. Such an arrangement is much more economical and much less prone to error. Its only possible drawback is that information must be transmitted, before the system begins to be built, about the particular connection which should be made and this must be done through the mechanism of genetic transmission in the case of the animal.

There must be some good reason why the system of genetic connection has not been preferred to a selection-through-experience principle in the case of imprinting. This may have something to do with one of the disadvantages of information transferred genetically. If a gosling were to be "instructed" genetically about its mother, it could only be instructed about *a* mother, not its particular mother. The genetic "message" is by its nature generic and unable to forecast the specific features of the goose mother. This then must be an important "consideration." A generic "image" of food is good enough for the goose, but apparently a generic image of mother is not. It would therefore seem that it is of the utmost importance to the gosling to recognize its own mother and not to confuse her with other female geese. The only way this can be achieved is through learning, or the selection of a message on the principle that it arrives at a certain time and under certain conditions and that it has certain general characteristics. The last proviso, "provided that it has certain general characteristics," may not be a real one. It may exist only apparently because the range of possibilities of selection may be limited to a certain number of "subscribers" or alternatives, and this would, of course, lead to economy in the size of the "exchange" or selecting system.

From this line of speculation it would appear that it is very important for the young of species which show imprinting not to confuse their parent with other possible parents. This in turn suggests that the parents themselves are somewhat selective and show aggression to the young of others. It would be interesting to test these suggestions empirically by attempting to correlate imprinting in the young with the characteristics of maternal care and aggression in the adult, the mobility of the young when it is still important for them to have maternal care, the chances of different broods becoming mixed, and so on.

It could be said that this line of thought shifts the problem one stage further back, namely, the selectivity of the parent. There seems no reason why the parent birds should be selective in the young they accept and, therefore, no reason why the whole system of imprinting should arise at all. The question which is really being asked is: "What are the disadvantages of a genetically carried gener-

[71]

ic image of a 'mother' in the young in a certain bird species?" One answer which springs to mind is that some mothers would be more like the generic image than others. A type of situation could arise which Tinbergen so excellently illustrates in the herring gull chick and its preference for a certain type of beak, and the oyster catcher with its preference for the larger egg. Some mothers would be overwhelmed by large flocks of young and other mothers deserted by their own young. This would have severe and somewhat comical disadvantages.

There is one other point which should be discussed. Thorpe (1956, p. 116) regards imprinting as generic. He says: "It is supra-individual learning—a learning of the broad characteristics of the *species*. . . ." Though he does not quote the evidence for this conclusion, we may presume that he bases it on an experiment by Hinde, Thorpe, and Vince, who studied the following response in moorhens and coots. These experimenters found that having learned to follow one artificial model, such as a black box, the young birds would also tend to follow another artifact, such as a red cane basket. But such generalization does not enable us to conclude that the learning of characteristics in their own species is similarly general and inaccurate. We might conclude that a European cannot recognize as individuals other Europeans because he is prone to confuse Chinese. As has been said above, the range of possible selection of characteristics which may be connected or learned is likely to be limited in the animal, for this leads to economy in the size of the selecting system. To make economy compatible with efficiency in learning accurately the characteristics of "mother," the alternative analyzers which it is possible to select to perform the discrimination from other possible mothers will not be selected at random from the classificatory mechanisms of the bird. They will be a small range of classificatory mechanisms, by selecting from which the bird will achieve the most efficient discrimination among birds of its own species. In this way a bird might be virtually "blind" to differences from an artifact to which it has been imprinted and generalize widely. However, such a bird might be exceedingly sensitive to differences among objects which it had been evolved to imprint on. As is shown by the writer (1957) in the case of nest-building in rabbits, "one may doubt the generality of conclusions about patterns of instinctive behaviour based on experiments in an environment in which the animals did not evolve."

[72]

VII

Extinction

Just as learning was ascribed to the sequential firing of two analyzers leading to the connection of their links to each other, so unlearning, or extinction, may be regarded as a failure of this sequential stimulation, after two links have become connected. When the environment alters after an order has been registered, the firing of one analyzer may not be followed by the firing of the subsequent analyzers in the row of links. It has already been postulated that the "threshold" of excitation of link x, the analyzer of which has fired, will rise in proportion with its control of motor output, if none of the analyzers attached to the links through which it is excited are fired. It is possible at this point to put the theory to experimental test in a situation where common sense would find it difficult to predict. The following deduction can be made from the theory. Suppose that a rat is trained in a T-maze with water in one goal box and food in the other. Suppose further that the rat was made alternately hungry or thirsty on successive trial series when it was inserted in the maze. If such a rat was prevented from entering the wrong goal box (for instance, the food box when it was thirsty) by a block which was invisible from the choice point, then such a rat should take longer to learn to go to the appropriate side than a rat without such a block, for the theory would predict that it is the first trial after a change of motivation which is disturbed.

The way the deduction is made is this. During the course of learning, two rows of links will be formed, one thrown into excitation when the animal is hungry and the other when it is thirsty (as in the case of the animals run by Kendler and discussed above in chapter iv). If by chance the animal goes up the wrong alley, then it will be met by a block (see Fig. 7). Then as the stimuli in that alley are not followed by the stimuli of the goal box, there should be a rise in the

[73]

threshold for the passage of excitation between the two links to which these analyzers are attached. As a result, when the animal's motivation is changed and the alley which had the block in it becomes appropriate, the threshold for the passage of excitation in the row subserving this alley will be raised. Consequently, there will be a greater bias for taking the inappropriate choice than in the rat which was allowed to wander into the goal box, only to find a reward which it did not want. However, if the animal, which found a block

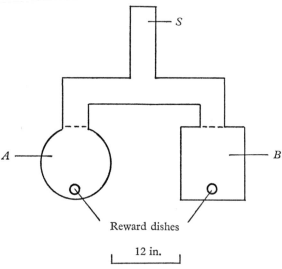

FIG. 7.—Diagram of the unitary-reward apparatus. *S*, starting alley; *A* and *B*, goal boxes. Broken lines at entrances to *A* and *B* indicate location of blocks when in position. For any given subject, the location of food and water in the maze is constant, food at one goal box and water at the other. When a member of the experimental group is motivated for the reward at one of the boxes, the path to the other is blocked. For the control group, neither path is blocked.

if it chose inappropriately on one day, does make the mistake on the next day toward which it has been biased when its motivation is changed, then it will again find a block and the threshold for the passage of excitation in the chain subserving this alley (which is now "inappropriate") will rise. Thus both chains should be affected, as the animal has now found blocks in both paths (before it finds again that one of them is unblocked). As the thresholds for the passage of excitation in a portion of both chains have risen, the animal should on the succeeding trial make a choice which is less biased toward one

[74]

side (as both sides are more equally biased). Consequently, after it has made a mistake, it should behave more like the control animals without blocks. Also it follows that the tendency to make a mistake should be strongest after a change of motivation. A full description of the experiment and the results are given elsewhere (Deutsch and Anthony, 1958).

The results of the experiment accord well with the theoretical prediction. We find that, if we take into account the first trials of the day only (in the first period of 24 days), the animals with blocks score about 62 per cent correct, whereas those without blocks score almost 79 per cent. Though this difference is highly significant statistically, that for all the trials taken together is not. An experiment by Hull (1933), analogous in conditions to that of the present experimental group, gave a similar result, as does that by the present author (1959), who also used a group analogous to the controls in the experiment under discussion. However, the rats in these experiments ran to the same goal box for both rewards. This complicates the interpretation of these experiments. They are discussed at length in the chapter on reasoning.

i

LATENT EXTINCTION

One of the consequences of the hypothesis which it is now possible to draw is that extinction and reinforcement of a habit (or response) can occur without its performance. The application of the theory in this respect will be made clearer if we use it to interpret a study of extinction by Seward and Levy (1949). In this two groups of rats, B and C, ran down an elevated pathway from a starting platform to a goal platform for a food reward. After some training, each rat in group B was placed on the goal platform with no food on it. The C group was identically treated except that it was placed on a strange platform. "Five such treatments were given. . . . On the following day all rats were given extinction trials to a criterion of two successive refusals to leave platform A (the starting platform) within three minutes. Group B reached the criterion in a mean of 3.12 trials, group C in 8.25; the difference was significant at the 0.01 level."

During the learning trials, it is assumed, a row of links becomes attached to the link whose analyzer fired when the rat found food. Nearest on the row to the links whose analyzers fired off in the presence of food would be links whose analyzers fired off in the

[75]

presence of the goal platform. When the rat finds itself on the empty goal platform, the analyzers signaling "goal platform" will fire and affect the link to which they are attached. The next link, to which analyzers signaling food are attached, are not similarly stimulated subsequently, as would be the case were the environment unchanged. This increases the "threshold" of excitation of the link to which the analyzers representing the goal platform are attached. As a consequence, less excitation would be passed to this link and through it to the links to which are attached analyzers representing the earlier portions of the pathway. Hence, the "habit" will run off at a decreased speed and show extinction with a repetition of this procedure. A habit can thus be weakened without actually having been elicited. This phenomenon has been called "latent extinction."

Moltz (1957) has recently proposed an explanation of latent extinction by an extension of the Hullian view. Before Moltz's suggestion, the Hullian view was that when a response is made, it sets up a tendency against being repeated, which is called "reactive inhibition" (IR). Usually this tendency for the response not to be elicited again by a stimulus is offset by an even greater tendency to be repeated which occurs if it is followed by a reward. When a reward does not occur, then the tendency for the response to be made simply diminishes. In Hullian language, reactive inhibition (IR) and conditioned inhibition (S^IR) are assumed to produce extinction by jointly opposing the reaction potential (S^ER). From this it can be deduced that a response must be made before it can begin to undergo extinction. However, there are cases in the literature (such as the experiment by Seward and Levy reported above) where responses do undergo extinction without having been elicited. In this experiment an animal's tendency to execute responses leading to the goal is reduced when it is placed in the goal and it is shown that this goal no longer contains the desired reward. The responses leading to this goal show a tendency to extinction even though they have not been executed.

Moltz attempts to explain these phenomena in terms of the function of antedating goal reactions. Hull suggested that the response made by an animal to the stimuli from the goal would tend to be elicited through the processes of conditioning by stimuli which precede the goal stimuli. However, this goal response made by an animal in the goal would only be made in a covert form before the goal was reached. Therefore there would be a goal reaction which he calls

[76]

an antedating or anticipatory one. This antedating goal reaction (r_g) when it is made generates proprioceptive stimulation, which is called s_g. Now these r_g-s_g combinations will become a part of the stimulus-response chain leading to the goal (Fig. 8). If S_c is "stimulus at the choice point" and R_r "the response of turning right," then in Figure 8 S_c evokes both R_r and r_g. In its turn r_g evokes s_g, which evokes R_r jointly with S_c.

Moltz suggests that latent extinction occurs when an animal is placed in an empty goal box where it has previously found reward, because antedating goal reactions occur repeatedly in the goal box. Because they are not reinforced after having been evoked, they undergo extinction, at least to some extent. Further, as these antedating goal reactions occur as components of the stimulus-response sequence leading to the goal, they will be aroused to a lesser extent

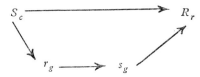

FIG. 8.—The stimulus-response chain used by Moltz

even at the beginning of this stimulus-response chain. If they are aroused but below their previous strength, the characteristic proprioceptive stimuli to which they give rise will diminish also. Therefore some of the stimuli which normally arouse the responses which lead toward the goal will be less intense, and this will produce less intense responses. In this way partial extinction can be explained on the r_g-s_g theory. This is made evident by referring to the example given. If the $r_g \rightarrow s_g$ component is knocked out of the illustrative diagram, then only S_c will be acting to evoke R_r.

The present theory does not depend in any way on response evocation. On this theory, extinction is brought about by the failure of one stimulus to follow another which has usually preceded it. Such a failure raises the threshold for motivational excitation to pass from the link joined to one of the stimuli to the other. As a consequence, all the cues on the side of the rise in threshold further from the source of motivational excitation (the goal) will diminish in attractiveness. For instance, if an animal is trained in a maze hungry, for a reward of food in the goal box, it can then, instead of being inserted in the start, be placed directly in the goal box. If we have taken the food out of the goal box, the animal will see that the cues in the goal box are no longer followed by food. This will cause a rise in threshold between the "goal-box" link and the "food" link. As a result, excitation which runs from the food link to the links underlying the beginning of the maze will be diminished in amount owing to the rise in threshold of the food–goal-box connection through which this excitation must pass.

Both theories could account for the data which existed on latent extinction when Moltz's suggestion (1957) was published. As a test to decide which was the more plausible, an experiment of the follow-

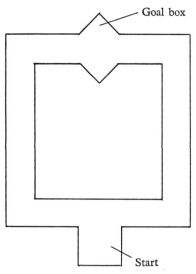

Fig. 9.—The maze used by Deutsch and Clarkson in the extinction experiment.

ing form was devised. (A full account is given by Deutsch and Clarkson, 1959c.) A maze in the shape of a square was made, in such a way that two alternative routes of the same length led to the same goal box, as shown in Figure 9. Doors were inserted just past the choice point and before the goal box on both sides to prevent retracing. The rats were then trained in this maze, having been made hungry for a reward of food in the goal box. They were rewarded whichever path they chose. After being thoroughly trained, the rats were prevented from obtaining the reward in the maze in two different ways. The first way was simply to leave the goal box

[78]

empty. Having made a response, the rat would not find it rewarded, as food was absent from the goal box. According to Moltz's view, the antedating goal reaction (r_g) should be evoked when the animal enters the goal box and should undergo partial extinction, as no reinforcement follows. This antedating goal reaction (r_g) which occurs in the goal enters equally as an ingredient into both the stimulus-response sequences. Hence this r_g-s_g component is removed from both the stimulus-response chains equally. Hence both chains should be equally affected if we take the r_g-s_g mechanism alone. However, the ordinary S-R mechanism will not be equally affected, where it is a different S-R chain, depending on the alley which is traversed. The R components of one of the chains only will have been performed unrewarded, and there then should be a tendency for the sequence which has been performed to be extinguished. Hence the animal, having run one way to the goal, should on the next run choose the alternative alley. (If it is objected that the r_g for both paths is for some reason not the same, then the same prediction still follows even more strongly. For then both the overt responses [R] and the antedating reactions [r_g] will suffer from reactive inhibition on one side only and not on the other.)

On the other hand, on the present theory no increase in alternation on the test trial would be predicted. The goal-box–food link connection would be common to both rows of links and therefore a rise in threshold in this connection would affect the excitation flowing through the goal-box–food links to both the rows of "alley" links equally. Therefore the attractiveness of the two alternatives at the choice point would not be differentially affected.

The second way of producing extinction was as follows. Instead of finding no food in the goal box, the animal found the entrance blocked from the path it had chosen to the goal box. This second experiment was performed only to make sure that the animals had in fact learned, that the animals were able to identify the two alternative pathways. It would have been difficult to be certain otherwise, as the animals were always given a free choice and rewarded for whichever alley they chose. (This control has the further advantage that it is theoretically similar to the experimental situation from the Hullian point of view, but entirely different on the present view.) The average number of alternations between the first two trials on the training runs was 8.8 out of a possible 19. When the goal box was left empty in the first test condition, the number of alternations (also out of a possible 19) was 9. However, when the path was blocked this number rose to 17 (again out of 19). In this way the prediction which was made from the present theory and tested in this experiment is borne out.

The present theory is also applicable to the kind of result obtained by Deese (1951). Deese trained his animals in a U-maze. They were rewarded in the box in one of the arms with food. After the initial training series, the experimental group was placed in the goal box after the food had been removed from it for four 1-minute periods. When these animals were afterward allowed to choose, they chose the side in which the food had previously been a smaller number of times than the control group. This group had not been placed in the empty goal box.

ii

EXTINCTION AND CONDITIONAL
LEARNING

The type of extinction treated so far has been where a constant conjunction between two cues has been followed by a constant lack of conjunction between them. First, cue b, whenever it occurs in the animal's experience, is followed invariably by cue a. Then, on the extinction trials, cue b is never, in the animal's experience, followed by cue a. The cases of learning dealt with and explained have also been instances where an animal was faced with a world in which the occurrence of a sequence of events was not dependent on the occurrence or non-occurrence of another event.

However, there are many cases where an animal can only expect a to follow b if, and only if, c occurs or if z does not. One of these cases occurs in Skinnerian conditioning. An animal is placed hungry in a box. There is a food trough and a lever which produces a click. It is given a reward of food in the trough only when it has heard the click. Having been thus rewarded a few times, the animal will begin to approach the trough even if it has heard no click. It has to learn that the trough contains food only when it has heard a click. Once this has been learned, the experimenter's task in training the animal is almost over. The animal will now repeat any action which produced the click. The difficult thing for the animal to learn is that the food-trough cue is followed only by food reward if, and only if, the click has occurred. The tendency to approach the trough, and to hover over it in the expectation of food, is very strong in the animal.

[80]

This tendency extinguishes during the course of successful training, but of course it remains extinguished only when no click has occurred, because as soon as the animal hears the click, or causes the click by depressing the lever, it will run to the food trough to find food.

First postulate.—We may therefore postulate that when the link y ("click") is stimulated by its analyzer as the resistance due to extinction between two links (x, "food," and z, "trough") decreases, this link will be connected to the link z ("trough"), whose resistance to excitation has decreased. This link y, which has been stimulated, will be attached in such a way as to inhibit the motor output of link z. This inhibition lasts until the analyzer attached to link y fires off. Then the stimulation of the analyzer attached to link z will (as usual) switch the excitation arriving at this link into the motor output. In this way the animal, having found food in the food trough in the Skinner box, will approach this trough when it is hungry. This will give rise to extinction of the attractiveness of the food trough. However, on one of these visits he will have just heard the click when he obtains food from the trough. The non-arrival of the click will hereafter inhibit the attractiveness of the trough (when the two links [y and z] are connected together). This inhibition will be removed when the click arrives. The animal will approach the trough and find food. Consequently the attractiveness of the trough will increase.

It has already been postulated that the threshold of excitation of a link the analyzer of which has fired will rise and that this rise will be proportionate to the control of motor output by this link, if it is not switched off. It follows, therefore, that links whose output is inhibited will not undergo this rise in threshold when they are not switched off in the conditional situation. Therefore the food-trough link will not undergo a rise in threshold if it is not switched off while its control of motor output is inhibited by the click link. A rise in this threshold will occur now only when the click link relinquishes its inhibition when a click occurs and no food is found in the food trough. On the other hand, if the click occurs and food is found in the trough, the threshold of the food-trough link is lowered. In this way, the original rise in threshold which occurred when the animal was not rewarded each time it approached the trough will disappear and the "habit" can rise to maximum strength even when it is not universally rewarded.

[81]

The phenomena of partial reinforcement can be interpreted in this light. An animal can be trained to repeat one action a number of times in order to secure a reward only once. For instance, a rat may be taught to press a lever a large number of times in order to obtain only one pellet of food at the trough. Even though a lever-press in this situation is rewarded more seldom than under the condition of one reward per lever-press, the responses are quite as vigorous and speedy and, further, extinguish less readily when reward is withdrawn. That is, an animal will execute more responses before it ceases to work than if it has been rewarded for every single response. The number of responses before extinction occurs tends to be proportionate to the number of times the reward should, on past experience, have appeared. It is not proportionate to the number of responses made.

This is held to occur in the following way. Suppose that there is a signal (or group of signals) generated, when an animal has performed an action such as a lever-press, a number of times, by an analyzer attached to some link. Suppose further that the animal obtains a reward only when it has performed this action a number of times. When the reward does not arrive, the threshold of the link underlying the action rises according to the rule for extinction. It is lowered when the reward arrives after the action has been repeated a number of times. The link, to which the analyzer signals the information about the number of times the animal has pressed since the last reward, is then attached to the link whose threshold is lowered, inhibiting the output of this other link as long as the signal from its own analyzer is not present. Consequently, no extinction of this other link can take place until the other link is stimulated by its analyzer. Extinction will take place only when there is a signal to the inhibiting link at the same time as there is no reward. Hence, a habit acquired under partial reinforcement will show a tendency to extinction, not in proportion to the number of unrewarded trials, but to the number of trials which the animal expected to be rewarded.

Second postulate.—We may postulate that there will be some signals which arrive just before or at the time when the threshold of a link rises because the analyzer of the link through which it is excited has not fired. The link x, whose analyzer x fired while the threshold of another link rose, will inhibit the motor output of any link while the analyzer x is firing.

In successive trials to extinction (where an animal is repeatedly trained to obtain a reward and then shown that the reward is unobtainable) the number of times taken by the animal before it ceases to try to obtain the reward steadily decreases. Here we may infer that a change in the situation due to the absence of the reward in the previous trial occurs when there is a rise in the threshold of a link. It will increasingly become a signal which will inhibit output from the various links while it is occurring. At the same time the occurrence of a reward in the previous trial will serve as a signal whose presence will disinhibit output as soon as it arrives (according to the first postulate). In these circumstances, the threshold of a link b, if its output is inhibited in the two ways postulated, will not be able to rise. (This is, of course, provided that the environment is left further unchanged.) It can only undergo diminution, if a follows b, if c and not if z. Hence maximal flows of excitation can be established between links a and b and the original rise in threshold disappears.

Such cases of restricted or conditional conjunction between cues are to be found in many situations which have been investigated with the aid of the Skinner box, such as discriminant conditioning (where an animal must learn to respond or not to respond according to the presence of some signal) and partial reinforcement (where the animal is rewarded only on a certain proportion of the trials). Other cases to which the above assumptions should be applied are such situations as detour problems, where an animal can obtain a reward only if it approaches the goal by going a longer way round.

An interesting situation of the conditional type involving a maze has been described by Elam, Tyler, and Bitterman. These experimenters, spacing their trials, gave 50 per cent random reinforcement on a runway. On the non-rewarded trial they used a white goal box and on the rewarded the rat ran to a black goal box (or vice versa). After this the animals were run without reward to either the black or the white goal box. As would be expected on the present theory, they kept on running longer to the color which had not been associated with reward.

VIII

The Hullian Derivation of Latent
Learning and Reasoning

Before proceeding to expand the hypothesis which has gradually been unfolded in the previous chapters to cover more complex phenomena, it may be well to examine the most widely accepted theory on the subject. Hull proposed his original derivation of reasoning in 1935. The proofs have recently been repeated by Hull himself (1952) and others to cover phenomena such as latent learning. To avoid the reproach of proposing explanations gratuitously when there are perfectly good ones available already, it is necessary to state in some detail why these previous explanations are unsatisfactory.

Freud's and Hull's methods of explanation are in many ways the same. Freud, extrapolating from the usual correlation between motive and action, postulates motives to account for behavior where no motive is obvious. Similarly, Hull, finding that the appearance of many responses can be correlated with stimuli, assumes that there are stimuli operating even where we cannot detect them. Both use a time-honored inductive technique in a similar way. "Where there is smoke there is fire. Therefore even if we can only see smoke, we can assume that there is fire too." To reason thus enables us to predict concerning conflagrations. It does not give us the mechanism of combustion. Hull, however, appears to be of the opinion that, when he introduces S_D, the drive stimulus, or r_g, the antedating goal reaction, he is suggesting a mechanism or in some way providing a mechanical or even physical explanation. Speaking of the fractional antedating goal reaction, he says (Hull, 1952, p. 350): "Further study of this major automatic device presumably will lead to the detailed behavioural understanding of thought and reasoning. Indeed the r_g-s_g mechanism leads in a strictly logical manner into what was formerly regarded as the very heart of the psychic. . . ." Freud, using the same logical technique, regarded his explanations as psychic.

Hull's belief that his theory in some way provides a mechanism can probably be traced to his view of the correlations which are inductively extended by him. To quote his first postulate, "Organisms at birth possess receptor-effector connections ($_sU_R$) which under combined stimulation (S) and drive (D) have the potentiality of evoking a hierarchy of responses that either individually or in combination are more likely to terminate a need than would be a random selection from the reactions resulting from other stimulus and drive combinations" (Hull, 1952, p. 5). These connections he considers "the body's first major automatic mechanisms for adapting to various types of emergency situations" (p. 348). However, all that Hull has said is that there are mechanisms or "connections" in the animal such that it will adapt. He has not told us what these mechanisms are and how they work. He has only told us what they do. That the animal adapts we know; that this could be done by a mechanism is merely a matter of faith. Hull certainly has not provided such a mechanism. He has merely expressed an observed correlation concerning the behavior of neonates in language which indicates that he believes a mechanism to be responsible.

Again the parallel with Freud is worth noting. Hull held that the observed correlations from which he inductively reasoned to unobserved events were somehow physical mechanisms. Freud in the same way began with correlations which he regarded as mechanisms of the psyche and so wound up with what he thought were psychic explanations.

Nevertheless, if we are clear about their logical status, such extensions of observed correlations as Freud's or Hull's can be exceedingly useful. If by assuming that empirical generalizations hold we are able to predict behavior at first sight outside their scope, we reduce the phenomena under consideration to a greater regularity.

It was one of the axioms of Hull's thought that behavior at any time is always the product of stimulation at an instantly preceding moment. Hence, if such stimulation is not observable it is assumed to exist. Such a situation arises in the case of behavior which is called motivated. When an animal is hungry its behavior undergoes a change. To Hull such a change must be the product of some stimulation. Accordingly, Hull postulates that there is a drive stimulus (S_D) operating. Further, he assumes that this inaccessible stimulus

[85]

will be correlated with other changes in the animal's behavior, in the same way as the observable events in its class. For instance, it will tend to evoke any response which it preceded when a reinforcement has occurred (Hull, 1952, Postulate III, p. 5).

There is another type of behavior which appears to be determined, not by stimulation impinging at the time, but by a distant goal. Here Hull suggests that a part of the stimulation characteristic of the goal is acting to determine the correct response. This raises a further problem. How is a part of the goal stimulation displaced? Hull again solves this by extrapolating from observed relationships.

> Consider an organism which is presented with a sequence or chain of external stimuli $S_1 S_2 S_3 S_4$ and S_G, and which makes a sequence of responses $R_1 R_2 R_3 R_4$ and R_G where S_G is the food stimulus and R_G is the consummatory response, e.g. that of eating. The organism is assumed to be hungry, so that S_{Dh} will accompany the R_{Ge} or eating response. The preceding considerations show that R_G may be reinforced to the persisting S_D and to the rather differently persisting traces of $S_1 S_2 S_3 S_4$ and S_G.

This is Hull's solution to the question: How is a part of the goal stimulation displaced? How, when it has been displaced, does it produce a performance leading to the goal?

It follows that on a repetition of this sequence there will be a tendency for S_D, together with the traces of S_1, S_2, S_3, and so on, to evoke R_G at the outset of the sequence and more or less continuously throughout it, except insofar as there may be a conflict between R_G and the necessary instrumental movements of the sequence, such as $R_1, R_2, R_3,$ and R_4. Presumably in any such situation the instrumental acts would dominate the conflicting portion of the antedating generalized act, permitting the non-conflicting or fractional portion to persist in a covert form (Hull, 1952, p. 125).

This fractional portion he calls r_G, which generates s_G. It occurs as a part of a chain of stimuli and responses which are reinforced, that is, close to the rapid diminution of the drive stimulus or to neutral stimuli that have themselves occurred close to such a diminution. The antedating goal reaction r_G and the fractional goal stimulus s_G thus obey the same rules as other stimuli and responses.

Hull was led into this extrapolation from the observed partly by his belief that this extension reduced the phenomena of insight and reasoning to the empirical relations to be found in simple forms of

[86]

learning. "The writer is inclined to the view that the principles of association between stimuli and responses, particularly as revealed in modern condition-reaction experiments, offer a possibility of explanation in a manner which Maier's analysis failed to take into consideration" (Hull, 1935, p. 221). Hull has been criticized on the grounds that his concept of the antedating reaction is vague. However, to say that a concept is vague neither destroys its usefulness nor gives grounds for its rejection. If by making such an assumption we drastically simplify the picture of animal behavior, we have some reason to believe that we are at least working on the right lines. This makes it likely that greater precision will emerge.

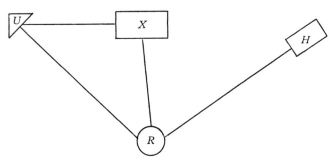

Fɪɢ. 10.—A diagram of the maze in Hull's adaptation of Maier's reasoning experiment.

Though their vagueness gives them a great deal of elasticity, Hull's assumptions, if consistently applied, do not in fact enable us to predict the phenomena of insight and reasoning, or even many forms of latent learning. This may be seen by examining some of Hull's explanations of these abilities.

Hull, in one of his papers (1935), attempts to reduce reasoning in the rat to principles of conditioning. He imagines a problem bearing some vague resemblance to Maier's (1929), and one which we have no evidence that the rat can solve. He then puts forward an analysis of the rat's successful solution.

There are four distinctive boxes, R, U, X, and H; as shown in Figure 10, R is connected to all other boxes and U is also connected to X. The animal is first to be trained hungry to go from R and U, separately, to X, where it is fed. Then it is to be trained to go from R to U and from R to H, as distinct habits for a reward of water. When the tendencies to go to U and H from R are equal, when the animal is thirsty, it is to be made hungry and placed on R with the path from R to X blocked. It is assumed that the animal would go to U and thence to X.

Briefly, Hull says that when the animal has been trained to go from U to X when hungry, hunger stimuli will tend to evoke the anticipatory reaction r_u. Further, when the animal is run thirsty from R to U, the platform R will tend similarly to elicit r_u, "brought forward to the beginning of the series presumably through its association with S_D or through the action of trace reactions while in

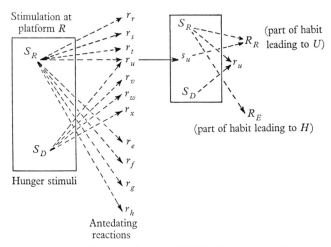

Stimulation at platform R

S_R

r_r
r_s
r_t
r_u
r_v
r_w
r_x

S_D

r_e
r_f

Hunger stimuli

r_g

r_h

Antedating reactions

S_R (part of habit R_R leading to U)

s_u r_u

S_D

R_E

(part of habit leading to H)

Fig. 11.—Annotated version of a part of Hull's diagram. The diagram represents the anticipatory goal responses which, according to Hull, would be aroused by S_R and S_D of hunger. R_R is the correct response and is evoked by s_u. The criticism is that if r_u is aroused by S_R, then s_u should have equally been conditioned to R_E during training.

their early stages (or both)" (Hull, 1935). Then when the animal is placed on R when hungry and path RX blocked, r_u will be evoked both by the S_D of hunger, and the stimulation at R, whereas all the other anticipatory responses (there are eleven on Hull's diagram) will have been elicited only by the stimulation at R (S_R). This will produce s_u, which in conjunction with S_R will produce the response R_R, which is a part of the response chain from R to U. The relevant part of Hull's diagram is reproduced in Figure 11.

Hull argues that R_E, which is a part of the response chain from R to H, will not be similarly evoked, because "it has only one excitatory tendency," that originating from S_R. This is not entirely true,

[88]

for S_R, according to Hull, arouses all the anticipatory components of the responses leading to H, which in turn evoke their appropriate stimuli. These, having occurred regularly in conjunction with R_E before the animal was rewarded at R_H, would tend to evoke R_E. However, s_u is stronger than these other stimuli, r_u being the product not only of S_R but also of the S_D of hunger. We may thus, with Hull, concentrate merely on r_u and s_u, and examine not solely the critical trials but also the training series to which he has not cared to apply his premises. Suppose (as Hull does) that the animal has already learned the habit segment U to X and R to U. Then r_u and s_u will occur, evoked by S_R and S_D, when the animal is placed thirsty on platform R and is then run to be rewarded at H; r_u and s_u will thus equally become a part of the initial part of the habit segment leading to H. In fact r_u will be present at R when the animal is being run to H from the very first trial. This cannot be the case when it first runs from R to U. Having been more often rewarded, the association should therefore be stronger between s_u and R_E than between s_u and R_R. Thus, if Hull predicts anything at all, he should predict that when the animal is placed hungry on R, it should run to H.

The objection applies equally if r_x has been conditioned back to occur at R, as in Osgood's account (1953). It seems that, on a strict interpretation of Hull, any antedating response, if it has been evoked, will become a part of any behavior segment, whatever reward it antedates. On the other hand, Hull, when he knows that the anticipation in ordinary parlance would be incorrect, tacitly applies the common-sense idea that an anticipation is reinforced only when it is confirmed, not rewarded. An interesting example is to be found in his last book, where he attempts to deduce another imaginary Maier-type experiment. Here both the strict rule and the common-sense version are applied at different points. If either version were to be used consistently throughout, the deduction could not be made.

To this example we shall now turn (Hull, 1952, p. 310). The animal is first trained to run from J to L (as in Fig. 12) for a very large food reward. Then it learns on a separate occasion to run from H to J for a small food reward, and subsequently from H to N for a similarly small food reward. Then it is placed hungry on H.

During the process of training from J to L,

the fractional goal response r_{Gee} first moves from L back toward J and then is evoked by J itself. Then when habit

[89]

H_1IJ is formed this rG_{ee}, now attached to J, becomes a part of J and is brought forward to path H_1. Thus a functional connection is established between the two related habit segments and becomes the basis of their subsequent unity [p. 311].

Here Hull assumes that rG_{ee} is reinforced in the same way as any other response, that is to say, if its occurrence is rewarded, it tends again to be evoked. Confirmation is not necessary for its reinforcement, nor will disappointment cause its extinction. If Hull assumed the opposite, rG_{ee} would not be brought forward to path H. If rG_{ee}

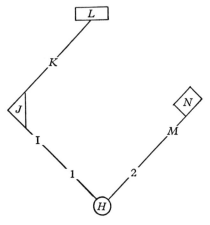

Fig. 12.—A diagram of the maze in Hull's adaptation of Maier's behavioral insight experiment.

functioned like an anticipation of L and the large reward there, it would be frustrated if it occurred when the animal was running from H to J. For it would subsequently find J, not L, and a small reward instead of a large one. Thus rG_{ee} would never be brought forward to path H because it would never be confirmed on this section, and if it occurred, it would suffer frustration which would presumably cause its extinction (Hull, 1952, p. 134). Therefore rG_{ee} is functioning like an ordinary R in this part of Hull's explanation and cannot be equated with anticipation in the way Hull identifies it in a section entitled "The Realization of an Anticipation and Its Frustration" (1952, p. 133). Hence Hull is able to say that two sets of antedating goal reactions will occur at H and through their intermediary stimuli tend to evoke the first response leading to J. As he assumes that

[90]

only one rG will be conditioned to the sequence leading to N, the animal should go to J. The deciding factor Hull stresses is the disparity in the number of bonds existing between the stimulation arising at H and the two behavior segments. However, Hull again appears to ignore the fact that, during training, the rG_e, belonging to J and rG_{ee} belonging to L would occur at H. It is to be remembered that the animal learned the two habits J to L and H to J before it was placed on H to learn to run toward N. Now rG_e and rG_{ee} ought to be evoked both because of the drive stimulus (S_D) of hunger and because of the stimulation arriving at H. Thus three antedating responses should be connected to the habit H to N.

Hull can escape this consequence only if he treats the rG's evoked at this point as expectations that would be falsified and subsequently extinguished on the animal's arrival at N. However, if he does this, he will not be able to use the argument which brings the anticipatory response belonging to L, rG_{ee} down to H, according to the argument outlined above. It is difficult to see any other reason for Hull's assumption that the antedating responses occurring at H would not be conditioned to the sequence H to N except that rG's function as expectations and not as responses; Hull never makes this reason explicit.

It might be open to him to argue that the stimulus situation at H is different when the animal is trained to N, and that therefore the antedating reactions previously evoked would be evoked more weakly. But, first, the drive stimulus S_D must be held to be the same. Consequently, the rG's antedating J and L will be evoked when the animal is hungry, possibly even if the animal is not started on H at all. Second, however weakly these rG's occur at the beginning of training to N at H, they will occur more strongly than at the beginning of training from H to J, and this path (H to N) will receive an *ex hypothesi* equal amount of reinforcement. Therefore, if anything, these rG's should, after such a propitious start, be more strongly conditioned to responses leading to N.

These are no isolated examples, such as might be due to an oversight. The antedating goal reaction has been treated as if it functioned as an expectation in other contexts. The inconvenient formal properties of an antedating goal reaction are forgotten when a prediction is required and "confirmation" is equated with "reward." An example of this may be seen in an analysis of the double-drive learning situation quoted with approval by Hull from Spence,

[91]

Bergmann, and Lippitt's discussion (1950) of an experiment by Kendler (1946).

Animals are trained while both thirsty and hungry to run a T-maze with water in one arm of the T and food in the other. In the test trial they are made either hungry or thirsty. Kendler found, under these conditions, a tendency to choose appropriately. The result is difficult for Hull to explain:

> If the animal turns right (R_{Rt}) to that arm of the maze, it finds food and eats; if it turns left (R_{Lt}) into that arm of the maze, it finds water and drinks. By analogy of the preceding analysis, S_{Dh} and S_{Dt} the drive stimuli of hunger and thirst will *both* be attached to R_{Rt} and R_{Lt}. So far as this mechanism alone goes, when the animal later enters the maze hungry but not thirsty the S_D alone will tend to evoke both R_{Rt} and R_{Lt} [Hull, 1952, p. 137].

Spence, Bergmann, and Lippitt attempt to give another analysis by introducing antedating goal reactions. ". . . the stimulus cues in the water arm and end box become, during training, conditioned to fractional anticipatory drinking acts (r_w) and, in turn, the proprioceptive cues (S_w) resulting from these anticipatory acts become conditioned to the response of entering this alley" (1950, p. 149). A similar conditioning of anticipatory eating acts will take place in the food alley.

> During the test series when only one drive is operative, the anticipatory act related to the goal for which the subject is motivated will, because of the greater strength of the particular drive stimulus, Hull's principle of stimulus dynamism, be much stronger (more vigorous) than the other, and hence will produce stronger proprioceptive cues. Thus, if the S is thirsty, proprioceptive cues from anticipatory drinking responses will be stronger than those from anticipatory eating. As these cues (S_w) will be conditioned to the response of entering the alley leading to water, they will tend to give this response the greater excitatory strength (stimulus dynamism) [1950, p. 549].

Now this explanation will not hold unless we treat anticipatory goal responses as expectations. In the above quotation it is assumed that the anticipatory goal responses of drinking and eating $(r_w$ and $r_f)$ occur at the choice point simultaneously. Therefore S_w and S_f are produced also. Hence, as S_{Dh} and S_{Dt} in Hull's analysis

[92]

quoted above, they should both be attached to the alternative responses. Consequently, one of them alone should evoke both the water- and food-turning tendencies. To say, as do Spence *et al.* (1950, p. 549), that "the relative excitatory strengths of the two competing responses will be a function of the relative strengths of the two fractional anticipatory goal responses" is manifestly incorrect unless it is tacitly assumed that only confirmation and not reward leads to the conditioning of an anticipatory goal reaction. This assumption is not stated and does not seem to follow in any way from Hullian theory. In fact, Spence *et al.*, in an analysis in the very next paragraph of the latent-learning experiment, explicitly make the opposite assumption. In this situation analyzed, an animal satiated for food and water is placed in a T-maze and finds water in one arm and food in the other and is then placed with its cage mates. Here

the fractional anticipatory goal responses are much weaker as the *Ss* do not actually eat or drink during the training period. The sight of food (or water) evokes conditioned fractional eating (drinking) responses. These, as described above, become conditioned to the cues of their respective alleys, *the reinforcement being provided by the social goal*, or possibly, as in higher order conditioning, by the sight of food or water itself (i.e., secondary reinforcement).

Here the assumption is clearly stated that anticipatory goal responses are reinforced by goals which do not confirm them. It may be noted in passing that this analysis founders on the same objection as the last.

It has been put to the writer that there are additional premises which could save the deductions that have been considered, even though they could not stand as they are. The failure is attributed not to Hullian theory but to a lack of explicitness in the argument. The point that should be made explicit in the above derivations is that goal responses are incompatible. For Hull, learning requires both S-R contiguity and reinforcement. If the final stimulus (S_F) is removed, so that R_F is blocked, some other incompatible response, R_X, must be made instead. This R_X, if reinforced, is carried forward as a fractional antedating r_x just as r_f was. The outcome of a competition between two incompatible reaction potentials is handled, in Hull's latest postulate set, by Corollary XIV, Postulate XIII. "When the net reaction potentials ($_s\bar{E}_R$) to two or more incompatible reactions (R) occur in an organism at the same instant, each in a magnitude greater than $_sL_{\bar{R}}$, only that reaction whose momentary reaction potential ($_s\dot{E}_R$) is greatest will be evoked" (Hull, 1952, p. 13). Anticipatory responses are presumably incompatible; since only one can be made at a time, they cannot both be equally reinforced in the same end box.

Though it would greatly decrease the plausibility of the derivations of latent learning and reasoning if they hinged on the assumption that antedating responses were incompatible, such premises might preserve the logic of the Hullian deductions. Let us, therefore, examine what their application would do to the argument, taking as an instance the Kendler double-drive situation, on account of its simplicity. Let us first of all take the training situation. The two factors to watch are the strength of the conditioning of the stimuli at the choice point (S_c) to the antedating goal responses (r_G), and, second, the strength of the conditioning of the fractional goal stimuli (s_G) to the responses of turning to either goal; only these factors can influence the final choice of the animal in the test, all others being equal according to Hull. Let us suppose that the animal is trained by turning an equal number (x) of trials to each side, the trials to each side alternating in equal numbers. Let us recall that the animal is trained while both hungry and thirsty to run for a reward to food on the left of a T-maze and to water on the right. Let us suppose that the strength of reinforcing factors on each side of the maze is balanced.

After a certain number of trials, one of the r_G's (let us say r_f) will be evoked by S_c, the stimuli at the choice point, owing to the fact that a set of trials to the food side occurred first in the training schedule. Suppose the number of trials in each set is x. Then r_f will be evoked by S_c x trials before r_w could be. Assuming an increment in the tendency of S_c to evoke r_F each time its trace is reinforced to R_f, r_f will have been strengthened x more times than r_w, its competitor, and therefore r_w could only be evoked by S_c x trials later than r_f (x trials is the very earliest, but it would probably be only later, as once r_f is evoked by S_c, other reinforcing factors begin to favor it). Then r_f will be evoked by S_c, at all events until the end of a set of trials to food, as the other r_G, r_w, cannot take its place because $S_c \rightarrow r_w$ is not increasing. We have already shown that r_w cannot take the place of r_f at S_c until at least x trials after r_f has appeared at S_c. But a set of trials is only x trials long. Hence r_w will

[94]

not appear during the set of trials, x in number, when the animal is running to water. Even if r_f does not increase appreciably while the animal is running to water during trials—as it ought, owing to reinforcement due to need reduction and secondary reward factors—it will at least hold the fort against r_w, which cannot appear till it is stronger than r_G. After the x trials, however, the siege is lifted, and r_G is enabled to get another x trials of increment. Thus r_w is never able to supplant r_f, even if we set the factors of reinforcement of $S_c \rightarrow r_f$ at the very lowest and make these vanishingly small.

Now if r_w is never evoked by S_c, s_w cannot be reinforced to a response of turning left. Hence, though r_w would be aroused at S_c if the animal was made thirsty alone, the stimulation s_w and S_c present at the choice point could not determine the correct direction except by chance.

If r_f is aroused and is stronger, whatever the reason (for instance, if the animal is made hungry), then the animal would most probably go to the water on the right. If an equal number of trials has been run to both sides, s_f will have been more frequently reinforced to R_{rt} on the water side. This is because s_f will only appear and be reinforced when r_f has been evoked by S_c, and this can only be during a set of trials toward the food. The probability is $1/x$ that r_f will appear on the first trial of a set of x trials toward food, and thus, given that x is greater than 1, the chances are that S_f will be reinforced fewer times toward R_{Lt} (the food side) than toward R_{rt} (the water side). The first set of trials toward water, after r_f has been evoked some time during the previous set toward food, will be a full one, and as the numbers of sets of trials toward each side are equal, s_f will be more frequently reinforced to R_{rt} (the water side), on the average. The probability of this will increase with x (the number of trials in a set). It is assumed in calculating this probability that the chances of the appearance of r_f are equal for any one of the trials (x in a set) toward food.

The above argument shows that an assumption of incompatibility of antedating goal responses does not help the derivations if the number of trials to each side is equal, and if they are made in equal batches. However, it might be said that an unfavorable training schedule has been chosen, and that a different type of training in which the numbers of trials are not kept rigorously equal, as between the sets of trials, could produce the desired learning in the animal. Let us therefore attempt to construct an optimum training

[95]

schedule, allowing ourselves complete freedom. The trouble with the equal sets of trials was that r_w did not get evoked at the choice point at all. In order to circumvent this, we must give the animal more trials in the set toward water after r_f has been evoked by S_c, so that r_w will be able to displace r_f at the choice point. In this way r_w will be evoked and will generate s_w, which will now be reinforced to the correct turn. But in doing this, we make the situation worse from another point of view. If we give more trials to water and continue until r_w is evoked by S_c instead of r_f, s_f will be more often reinforced to the response of turning to water (R_{rt}). Thus the tendency of s_f to be reinforced to R_{rt}, already present when the trials were precisely equated, will be aggravated. Thus if we wish $S_c \rightarrow r_w \rightarrow s_w \rightarrow R_{rt}$ to take place at all we must inevitably strengthen $S_c \rightarrow r_f \rightarrow s_f \rightarrow R_{rt}$ over $S_c \rightarrow r_f \rightarrow s_f \rightarrow R_{Lt}$. If we do not, $s_w \rightarrow R_{rt}$ will never occur.

We are thus caught on the horns of a dilemma. It must also be clear that further training will not help. If we wish to strengthen $s_f \rightarrow R_{Lt}$ we must first evoke $S_c \rightarrow r_f$. To do this we must reinforce $s_w \rightarrow R_{Lt}$, since, when we run the animal to food, r_w will first be evoked at S_c, as it has a larger reaction potential. It is stronger in virtue of the number of trials on which the trace of S_c was reinforced to R_w in the goal box, and any reinforcement which occurred when S_c evoked r_w—all after r_w had drawn even with r_f and had displaced it at S_c. Now for r_f to appear at S_c, it must take at least the number of trials to the food side which occurred after S_c had evoked r_w when the animal was running to the water side. That means, however, that s_w will now be more strongly reinforced to R_{Lt} than to R_{rt} (water side). This will not give the correct prediction.

In the preceding discussion it has been assumed that the reinforcement of the trace of S_c to R_f or R_w is more effective than the reinforcement of S_c to r_f or r_w. In fact, the reinforcement of S_c to r_f or r_w has been set at a minimum. If, however, it is made larger than the reinforcement to the trace, the argument becomes somewhat simpler. Once an r_G is evoked and reinforced to the stimulus which evoked it, over r_G's simply cannot displace it. Each time the trace of this stimulus becomes reinforced to other responses, the bond of the stimulus itself to the r_G will always undergo a large increment.

Another objection has been made against the preceding criticism. It has been said that the present writer assumes that in the examples

[96]

discussed there is only one stimulus combination (S_c) at the choice point that gets conditioned to responses on both sides. But actually the stimulus traces conditioned to the two r_G's are not the same. If food is on the right and water is on the left, then r_f and r_w are conditioned to different sets of place cues and response cues; viz., those on the right and left, respectively. It is true that Hull did not make this distinction in his 1935 article. But in 1952, paraphrasing the Spence, Bergmann, and Lippitt analysis, he did distinguish clearly between "the stimulus traces of . . . looking right at the choice point x of the $T(S_{xR})$ and beyond and the trace of S_{xL} (looking to left at choice point x)." As a result, his ensuing derivation seems to avoid the difficulties brought up.

It is true that some stimulus traces will tend more strongly to evoke antedating eating responses, and others antedating drinking responses, in the Kendler type of situation. Once the animal has made the response which will make the appropriate, more strongly conditioned, stimuli impinge on its receptors, there is no longer a problem. Why should the animal choose to expose itself to one set of stimuli rather than the other? Looking right or looking left will exclude one set of stimuli. However, both sets of stimuli will tend, owing to previous learning, to evoke a response, though one more strongly than the other. If the choice is random, the animal will expose itself to either set of stimuli indifferently. Once one set of stimuli is made to appear in such a way that the other set will concomitantly disappear, the animal's behavior will be determined by it. Thus if the animal looks at the weaker set, it does not help to say that the other set would be stronger if the animal looked at it, for it is the set that is impinging which is at that moment stronger. It is the actual present stimuli that should determine the response, and not some other hypothetical ones, which would be stronger if only they were impinging. The stimuli from both sides which occur concomitantly will tend to arouse both r_G's equally, as they occurred together during training. These occur up to and at the choice point. The animal's behavior at the choice point cannot be governed by stimuli which it has not yet received. It is unlikely that Hull himself would have wished to take this line of defense. If we assume a differential exposure to stimuli from one side, we do not need to have an explanation in terms of r_G's. The orthodox conditioning explanation which he rejects would do just as well.

Though the above examinations of lines of defense has produced nothing positive, it has at least clarified the issue. It is not sufficient for the appropriate antedating goal reactions to be evoked in the crucial trials; the fractional goal stimuli to which they give rise must also have been conditioned to the correct response. What is needed is some mechanism which prevents the inappropriate antedating response from occurring, if the subsequent goal response is not like it. This can be ruled out. Alternately, there must be some mechanism which prevents the association of a fractional goal stimulus with a subsequent response, if the subsequent goal reaction is not the full version of the antedating reaction which gave rise to the fractional goal stimulus. However, such a mechanism could only work if assumptions of incompatibility of antedating goal responses were *not* made. Another way, and perhaps the most plausible, is to assume that only the correct antedating goal response is reinforced. Again it must be assumed that antedating responses are not incompatible. As these last two suggestions would involve closely similar assumptions, they will be discussed together.

An explicit introduction of these assumptions of confirmation into Hullian theory would raise considerable problems. And yet these must be faced. For if the above examination of the Hullian use of the anticipatory goal response is correct, many important derivations will not stand unless these assumptions are explicitly introduced. The problem may best be outlined by considering a concrete example. Suppose a child expects some ice cream but instead is rewarded by being given a shilling; then if its expectation functions as a response, the next time in the same situation the child should expect ice cream even more strongly. Further, when it becomes hungry for ice cream, it should tend to behave in such a way that it will be brought into the situation where, expecting ice cream, it received a shilling instead. In order to avoid such predictions, it must be stipulated that an anticipatory response will be reinforced only if it is followed by another response like itself. However, this other response must not be an anticipatory response because, as we have seen, anticipatory responses are evoked somewhat too frequently.

This means that there must for the animal be some way of distinguishing anticipatory responses from other responses. This separation of real responses from make-believe or anticipatory responses is also made necessary on another ground. Real responses must presumably be reinforced without the recurrence of another response like themselves.

[98]

Yet, if the anticipatory responses are in a different class from real or actual responses, in what does their similarity consist? Are they copies occurring in some special part of the musculature or in the central nervous system? Or are they muscular contractions carrying out a special coding?

Further, granted that a satisfactory way of differentiating them is proposed, what leads to their initial differentiation when they are evoked? It has been supposed by Hull that an anticipatory goal response is evoked in identically the same way as any other response. What, then, will determine, when a response is evoked, whether it will be classed as anticipatory or actual? This classification is necessary for the correct formula for reinforcement to be applied.

It seems, however, that even if the relevant premises were included in Hullian theory, and contradictory premises removed, its scientific status would be impaired. As we saw earlier, one of its claims to scientific usefulness was that it reduced complex phenomena to simpler observed correlations. Now, however, the complex phenomena would be introduced in their own right to lead an uneasy coexistence with the simpler phenomena. The theory would become little more than a clumsy redescription of facts it dealt with.

To conclude and sum up, we can say that many of the Hullian derivations concerning reasoning and latent learning which use the antedating goal reaction (or the anticipatory goal response) are not logically sound and that the oversight is of the following nature: In the usual instance an antedating goal reaction (r_g) will undergo extinction if the goal reaction of which it is a fraction does not occur and provide reinforcement. For instance, an antedating food response will be weakened if the animal is no longer rewarded in the goal box. But suppose that instead of a mere withdrawal of food, another reward occurs instead. The antedating response to food, having been evoked, will now continue to be reinforced. In the derivations examined, Hull appears to overlook that the antedating response would continue to be reinforced to the "wrong" goal if the goal reward changed, and so extends the case where reward is withdrawn to the case where it is substituted. This extension is warranted neither by the premises used in the derivations nor, as far as the writer can see, by anything in Hull's system. However, it seems that Hullian theory, if it is to be persuasive, must be more explicit in these derivations either by showing how its present suppositions may be used or by introducing fresh assumptions.

[99]

The only way that the writer has been able to explain the consistent illicit reasoning when anticipatory goal response is used, is to assume that having explained the formation of anticipations and their frustrations in the simple case, Hull assumed that he could explain more complex cases of anticipatory phenomena. Confirmation and reinforcement are coextensive when an anticipatory goal response of food is subsequently reinforced by food in the goal box. Similarly frustration and extinction are coextensive when an anticipatory goal response is not followed by reinforcement. But confirmation and reinforcement are not coextensive when an animal which is both hungry and thirsty makes an anticipatory response characteristic of eating but is rewarded by water instead. Here the anticipatory response is reinforced but the anticipation of food, in ordinary language, is frustrated. The simplest way to explain the Hullian error is to assume that the everyday meaning of anticipation has slipped into Hull's thinking, where only the technical connotation is warranted.

IX

Insight, Reasoning, and Latent Learning

Animals under some conditions can draw upon past experience acquired on diverse occasions to solve a problem without trial and error. When the problem is not a novel one, we say that the animal has learned and we point to a process of trial and error which took place when the problem was new. These situations have been dealt with in a previous chapter. There are, however, cases in which the animal solves a novel problem without trial and error, though it draws upon information about the situation acquired on previous occasions, perhaps under conditions of different motivation and reward. These cases are called instances of latent learning and reasoning. We talk of reasoning when the animal has to combine two sets of information in some way in order to find a solution. All the information which the animal must utilize in order to solve the problem is never presented together. The animal is then set a goal which it can reach without error only by "putting together the various pieces of knowledge." In latent-learning experiments the situation with which the animal is confronted is similar. The difference lies in the fact that all the evidence which the animal will need to use in order to reach the goal which will be set it is presented together, sometimes in the order in which it will occur in the test and sometimes in an order determined solely by the random explorations of the animal in the maze and the random selection of points of entry and exit by the experimenter.

The word "insight" has been variously used. It has been spoken of in connection with such things as taking short cuts. It has also been used where an animal solves a problem without trial and error when it has not been presented with the relevant information previously by the experimenter as in the latent learning or reasoning situation. Because of this omission, it has sometimes been supposed that the animal has in fact solved problems without ever having been presented with the relevant information. If we make this assumption, it must be either that the animal has been so constructed that the information which it needs is already supplied by hereditary factors—in which case the label "instinct" is appropriate—or that the solution is purely accidental. It seems, however, more plausible to believe that in these cases of "insight" the information, though not presented by the experimenter, has been previously acquired piecemeal on diverse occasions (cf. Birch). If this argument is accepted, then the problem of insight reduces to the same as the problem of latent learning and reasoning, defined above.

A theory of learning and performance under goal-seeking conditions has already been put forward in a previous chapter.

As the same system will be used to account for the types of ability described above, a more formal résumé of the theory will be given. The rules under each number are not necessarily independent axioms. They have been numbered merely for ease of reference.

The system is made up of five elements. These elements are fully defined by the relations between themselves and other elements. Only some of them can be given a physical identification at present. These elements are called (a) analyzer (to be identified with a receptoral system), (b) a link, (c) a motor (or effector organization), (d) an environment, (e) a feature of the internal medium (to be identified with a hormone, etc.). What these elements are in themselves need not be asked. They can all be considered the same, differing only in the way that they are connected to, and affect, the others.

The relations obtaining between these five elements could be reduced to two. These are (1) increasing excitation, (2) decreasing excitation. (The case of the relations to environment is more difficult logically, though it offers little difficulty in practice.)

The following are the rules of the system:

There exist in the nervous system units consisting of three elements connected together—links, analyzers, motor systems.

1. One element, to be called a link, is connected to a receptoral system, called an analyzer.

2. In the case of certain links, to be called primary, these are set

into excitation by a feature of the internal medium (for instance, alteration in osmotic pressure) in proportion to its magnitude.

3. A primary link is connected to certain receptoral mechanisms to be called analyzers. When these analyzers are stimulated, the sensitivity to excitation of these primary links by the internal medium decreases.

4. A primary link is not itself directly connected to the motor system. It is instead connected to a secondary link which receives its excitation from the primary link.

5. This secondary link is attached to the motor system and to an analyzer. A secondary link when it is excited by a primary link, and its analyzer has been stimulated, will persist in exciting the same part of the motor system and maintain the same movement pattern, while the input from the analyzer attached to it increases. When there is a decrease, its motor output will vary and it will alter its movement pattern. A link will thus tend to maximize its own stimulation.

6. This secondary link may also be attached to another secondary link, to which it will transmit the excitation which it receives from another link (primary or secondary).

7. (a) This excitation will be transmitted only until the analyzer attached to the link is stimulated. When this analyzer is stimulated, the excitation reaching this link will then be switched to control the motor system and the link will act to maximize its own stimulation by the analyzer (according to 5). (b) Even when its analyzer has ceased being stimulated, the link which has stopped transmitting excitation because its analyzer was stimulated will take some time before it will transmit excitation in the same proportion as before its analyzer was stimulated.

In this way, excitation will be passed from link to link until a last link is reached or until a link is reached whose analyzer is undergoing stimulation. Here the motor system will be excited, and the excitation will be conveyed to no further links. The simple system which has been set up either through learning or through genetic factors could function in this way, but it is assumed that the cues which set off the analyzers in this system are fed in strict sequence, one after the other. This is an idealized situation. Often two or more cues will be impinging on the animal at the same time. When simultaneity, instead of succession, occurs, a different connection will occur (dealt with in rule 9).

[103]

Prior to learning, most of the secondary links will not be attached to other links but only to analyzers and the motor system.

8. When there is a link whose analyzer is stimulated, another link, the stimulation of whose analyzer has just ceased, will be attached to this first link, so that this first link will transmit excitation to it. Thus temporal succession of the stimulation of analyzers by cues will lead to an ordinal proximity of attachment when the row of links is formed. (This arrangement will be called "links in series.")

9. (a) When there is a link whose analyzer is stimulated during the whole time the analyzer attached to another link is being stimulated, then these two links will form an inhibitory connection (this being called a connection in parallel). One link will inhibit the passage of excitation through the other. A link will inhibit another, depending on how much it is being inhibited itself in this manner. If a link is connected in this way only to one other, we shall assume that it cuts down any excitation in this link by a half. If it is connected in this way to two others, which are themselves not connected to each other, or others, in this way, then when it is excited it will inhibit either of the other two, when they are excited proportionately less, and they will inhibit it more. In this way the excitation conveyed down a series of links will tend to be constant, however many links there are in parallel at any one point. Hence for most purposes of prediction, we can assume that only a simple series arrangement is operating, with a complex cue at each point. (b) If there is only a partial overlap of the duration of two analyzers being stimulated, a series arrangement of the two links concerned will occur.

10. (a) As each analyzer is thought of as having only one link, once an order of stimulation is already recorded, the order of connection between the links cannot be reduplicated. (b) Also, if an analyzer attached to a link in the middle of a recorded sequence is touched off, another link (whose analyzers fired off and which was not previously a part of that sequence) will be attached to this first link either in series or in parallel, depending on the temporal relations of the stimulation of the two analyzers. (Rule 10b can be deduced from 8 and 9.) When a sequence has been set up, the environment may alter. Then one analyzer may not be succeeded by a firing of the next.

11. The threshold of excitation of the link x, the analyzer of which has fired, will rise if the analyzer attached to the link nearer

the source of excitation does not fire. And this threshold will continue to rise while this switching-off is delayed. This rise will be proportionate to the amount of control by the link of the motor output.

Thus, when the first link in the row is again excited on a subsequent occasion, the amount of excitation transmitted to the link x and from it to its neighbor and so to the rest of the row will be diminished.

12. Each link has a certain "threshold" of excitation. Because of this each link will pass on less excitation than it receives. This "threshold" of excitation of a link will be lowered each time a link is switched off. The lowering of the "threshold" will be proportionate to the intensity of excitation present in the link at the time. One of the consequences is that the more often cues arrive in the recorded sequence, the more excitation will be passed through the row of links when it is again excited.

13. If there are two or more rows of links excited, the links at the end of the rows may be setting off movements that are incompatible. In this case the link with the highest rate of excitation will determine the movements.

Hence, as a deduction from rules 12 and 13, when two links are setting off competing actions, the one which has fewer links between itself and the first link will obtain precedence, other things being equal. There will frequently arise occasions on which one link will be found to be a member of two or more different rows or series of links. A cue will have been noticed which is common to two or more situations at once.

14. When a link is a member of two or more rows at once, the excitation which it receives will be passed through it from one row that may be excited to another row of which it is a member. (It will transmit its excitation to its neighbors according to rule 6.) The greater the proportion of links which two rows have in common at one point in the sequence, the greater the transfer of excitation from one to the other at that point in the sequence. This is subject to one limitation derivable from rule 9. If a link is a common member of two rows or series, the amount of excitation that it will transmit will be the smaller the greater the number of links to which it is joined in parallel. This means that if there is a cue which is occurring concomitantly with a great number of other cues in various situations, the less excitation will be passed through it from a row or series

[105]

representing one situation to the others. On the other hand, cues which are more unique will transfer excitation more efficiently.

A similar deduction can be made even where no transfer of excitation is involved. The cues in a situation which are concomitant with cues in other situations will determine the animal's behavior less than the cues which are more "unique" and it will be these more unique ones which will determine the animal's behavior to a greater extent. The links underlying these cues will be passing more excitation.

(For the sake of graphic convenience, when there are many links common to two rows, they will be represented just as a single link. This link, according to the proportion it actually represents, will be spoken of as transmitting more or less excitation according to a rough criterion of similarity between the rows, bearing in mind the proviso from rule 9 just mentioned.)

i

INSIGHT AND REASONING

Having set up this comparatively economical system we are now in a position to examine how it would explain some of the evidence. Let us begin by taking an experiment originally performed by Tolman and Honzik, and S. Evans, and more recently repeated by Caldwell and Jones in an inclosed maze. We have Osgood's word for it that, if this is a case of reasoning, it is one to which a Hull-type analysis would not be applicable unless it was shown to be an artifact of the method of testing. In the experiment of Caldwell and Jones, the rat was taught three paths to the same goal, a straight alley and two other paths. One of these was much longer than the other and joined the straight alley nearer the goal than the other detour path. After training, the straight alley was blocked at a well-demarcated point before the longer path joined the straight alley but after the shorter detour had already met it (Fig. 13). The rats after this experience of the block mostly chose the longest path, the only one which the block did not affect.

Assume that three rows of links were formed during the process of learning the three alternative pathways. According to the hypothesis put forward, the analyzers attached to a row of links and their order correspond to the cues picked up by the rat and their order in each alley (rule 8). However, as reduplication of an order already

[106]

laid down does not occur, those parts of each path which overlap are all represented by the same row of links (rule 10). Three parts of the paths which do not overlap are arranged on separate rows (rule 8). One of these three parts will be represented on the same row as the common part of all the paths. The other two parts will be organized on separate rows and connected to the row representing the path learned first via common links (10b). When the animal finds that the straight alley to the goal is blocked, then, according to rule 11, the threshold of excitation of the link x, the analyzer of which has fired, will rise if the analyzer attached to the succeeding link does not fire and will continue to rise while this switching-off is delayed. Now both the straight alley and the shorter detour have that portion of

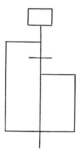

Fig. 13.—A schematic drawing of the maze originally used by Tolman and Honzik.

the runway in common in which the block is inserted. This means that both paths have this portion represented on the same row. Now when this sequence does not recur, there will be a decrease in the excitation which is transmitted past the point where the break in sequence occurred. Consequently, when the animal is again at the choice point, it will tend to go via the path which is "represented" by that row of links in which there is no impediment to the transmission between the link representing the choice point and that representing the goal. For, according to rule 13, if there are two or more rows of links excited, the link with the highest rate of excitation will act on the motor system. Hence the rat will choose the longest detour.

Hull has attempted to explain some of N. R. F. Maier's experimental data on reasoning. He uses a schematic form of the sort of situation that Maier used. (The same form will be used here only to invite comparison.) Four goal platforms are used, R, U, X, and H. R is connected with every other box and U is connected to X (see Fig. 14). The rat is then trained to run from R to X for a reward of food. Following this it is trained to go from U to X for a food reward and from R to U and R to H for a water reward, in that order. We may assume that, after he has learned, the tendencies to go to U and H when placed thirsty on R are equal for the rat. In the crucial trial the animal is placed hungry on R with the path to X blocked. There is then only one way to X and this is through U. The rat has never been this way before in any one trial. However, let us assume

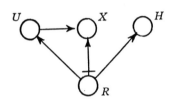

Fig. 14.—A diagram of the problem envisaged by Hull

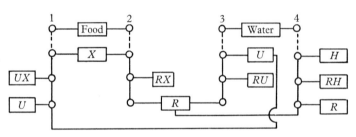

Fig. 15.—The effect of Hull's proposed experiment on the postulated system.

that rats can synthesize their partial experiences, and that they run toward U, and then to X, more frequently than to H.

Assume that four rows of links have been formed during training, each consisting of four links. (This number is arbitrary and adopted for the sake of simplicity.) Many more links are actually held to intervene between those represented. These may be represented as in Figure 15. The first row has an analyzer which responds to food attached to its first link, then an analyzer set off by a feature on platform X. There follows UX, an analyzer set off by a landmark between U and X and then U, an analyzer representing platform U. The other rows in the diagram are to be similarly interpreted.

[108]

When the animal is made hungry, rows *1* and *2* will be excited according to rules 2 and 6 (rule 2, "In the case of certain links, to be called primary, these are set into excitation by a feature of the internal medium . . . in proportion to its magnitude," and rule 6, "This secondary link may also be attached to another secondary link, to which it will transmit the excitation which it receives from another link [primary or secondary]). This excitation will be transmitted to row *3* via the common link U and to row *4* via "water" link (rule 14, "When a link is a member of two or more rows at once, the excitation which it receives will be passed through it from one row that may be excited to another row of which it is a member"). We may neglect for the purpose of this explanation the excitation transmitted via the link R to rows *3* and *4*, as the excitation will not be transmitted to the link to which analyzer R is attached in row *2* as soon as $RX;$ a cue between R and X appears (rule 7) when the animal is placed on the platform R, assuming that RX is in front of the block. The amounts of excitation at the links to which analyzers RU, RX, and RH are attached are unequal, as more links intervene between RU and the source of excitation than RX, and RU than RX (rules 12 and 13). The animal will accordingly approach RX (rule 13). As there is a delay in the appearance of X owing to the block, excitation at the link to which the analyzer RX is attached will decrease (rule 11) and the link to which analyzer RU is attached will begin to determine output, as there are fewer links between RU and the source of excitation (via U) than between RH and the source of excitation (via U, excitation via R having been temporarily interrupted). Hence the animal will take the path leading to U and thence to X.

From a comparison of this explanation with that of the experiment on page 115 it will be seen that success in solving the problem should occur only if there is a sufficiently large difference in the number of links between U and RU, on one hand, and U and RH, on the other. Translated into experimental terms, the platforms should be large and well furnished with many cues, so that the "psychological" distance between the water cups and the two alleys is made large. Unless this condition is met, success in Hull's "conventionalised version" would not be expected to occur. The use of blocks in the alleys should also be avoided (see Deutsch and Anthony, 1958, and also chap. vii).

Unfortunately, this prediction does not differentiate between this theory and Hull's. Hull's explanation of this fictitious experiment is fallacious (chap. viii).

ii

A REASONING EXPERIMENT

At this point a test of the present hypothesis concerning reasoning is reported. A problem was devised in which alternative solutions were admissible, so that we could see what the problem looks like to the animal and not only whether it can solve it. Such a problem is also a more searching test of a theory, as the theory must not only predict that a solution should occur but which solution should occur.

A problem of the following nature was set the animal (Deutsch and Clarkson, 1959b). A maze was used (see Fig. 16) in which there

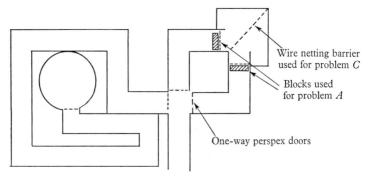

Fig. 16.—The apparatus used for the reasoning experiment

were three alleys between which it could choose at the choice point. Two of these alleys were of equal length and led to the same goal box. The third alley was much longer and led to a second goal box. The animal was introduced into a maze hungry and rewarded for whatever choice it made in one of the two goal boxes. Both the boxes and the alleys were differentiated in various ways. After the rat had become thoroughly familiar with the maze after many days' training (18 days before the first test with three trials a day), the animal was set its first problem. There were three problems with which the animals were presented in this maze. The first was to leave the nearest goal box empty and to see what the animal would do on the trial after it had found this change. It was fortunate that all the animals were in the habit of running to the nearer goal box almost invariably on the first run of the day, taking one of the short

[110]

alleys. Having found this near goal box empty, the rat can on the next trial either repeat its choice, take the other path leading to the same box, or choose the path leading to the more distant goal box. Common sense and theory agree in predicting that it is in fact this last choice which will be made. In fact, nine of the twelve animals which were used chose the long alley. The probabilities of such a result occurring by chance is rather lower than the figures suggest. Many of the rats had by the eighteenth day formed rather set habits, for the succession of each day's choices had become fixed. Hence the rats' deviation from their set routine on the test day lends more significance to the obtained result. (For a more detailed discussion of the statistics and tables of choices see Deutsch and Clarkson, 1959*b*.)

The second problem which we can set the animal, once it is trained, is to insert a block in one of the shorter alleys which it always chooses first. (As a matter of fact, both short paths were blocked as a matter of experimental convenience, but of course the rat would only find out about the block it ran into.) To find food, the animal can do either of two things. Either it can take the other short path which leads to the near goal box or it can go to the more distant goal box. On the present theory, in a way to be shown later, it is predicted that the animal should take the other short path. Again nine of the twelve animals chose this path, and again the probabilities of this occurring by chance were very low, taking the animals' previous habits as a guide.

The third problem with which the animals were faced was a wire-mesh barrier placed diagonally across the nearer goal box with the food perceptible to, but not edible by, the rat. The rats were on all occasions watched and were not removed until they had made unmistakable attempts to thrust their snouts through the mesh to reach the food. In this way the situation was made different from the one in the first problem, where the animal found no food. In this situation, the animal can again do either of two things to obtain food. Either it can run up the other short path to reach the food on the other side of the barrier or it can go to the more distant goal box. The present theory would predict that the animals should choose the distant goal box. Again, nine of the twelve animals set this problem did so, with a low probability that such a result should occur by chance. As such a result is not what most people would predict by common sense, it greatly strengthens belief in the theory.

[111]

The situation itself which was chosen is superior in some respects to problems where the environment is varied only in one way within one experiment. A change in response following the setting of a problem, however universal it is in the rat population, does not necessarily betoken a solution of the problem (cf. S. Evans). It may merely indicate the stereotyped reaction to change in environment constituting the experimental conditions. However, if various problems are set, it is unlikely that the changes occurring in behavior are all due to differing reactions which are all only accidentally solutions.

According to the present theory, three rows of links will have been formed in the order that the receptoral structures, detecting the cues in the three paths, and attached to each link, have been stimulated.

The two paths leading to the same goal box will have many links in common near the link which is excited by a food deficit. The path which is the longest will be the least preferred (according to rules 12 and 13) as there will be the larger number of links between the choice-point link and the source of excitation. If, however, one of the shorter paths to the same goal box has already been chosen immediately before, then the probability of the longer path being chosen will rise (according to 7b).

When the near goal box is left empty, then the stimuli of this goal box are not followed by food as in training, whichever of the two stimulus sequences we take. Hence (by 11) the threshold of excitation of the links conveying excitation to the choice-point units of the two shorter paths will rise. Therefore the excitation of the choice-point unit belonging to the longer row of links will rise in relation to the choice-point links of the two shorter rows. Consequently there will be a greater likelihood of the longer path being chosen. This is what emerges from the experiment. We should predict that the likelihood of the longer path being chosen depends on the relation of its length to those of the short paths.

When a short path is blocked, the stimuli in this path are not followed by the stimuli of the goal box. The break here is occurring in only one of the stimulus sequences. The other is left unaffected. Hence the excitation traveling down the other two rows of links will be the same, relative to each other. As more excitation is reaching the end of the shorter row, this row will determine the behavior of the animal. The rise in threshold due to the block will occur only in one row (according to 11). The other short path will be chosen, as in the experiment.

When a wire mesh is inserted in the middle of the goal box, preventing the ingestion of food, the stimuli of the entry to the goal box from one side will not be followed by the stimuli of eating. Hence there will be a rise in threshold in the row of units underlying this sequence. However, there are many stimuli in common here in the two sequences leading to the ending at the same point—stimuli emanating from the same goal box entered from two different directions. Therefore some of the links will be the same, and these will undergo a rise in threshold (according to 11). Hence in the row representing the other short path there will also be a lessening of the excitation transmitted proportionate to the number of cues common at the stage where the mesh occurred. Therefore, if the overall similarity is large and the long path not too long, the animal should choose to go to the distant goal box rather than to the other half of the near goal box where it has just seen food. The experimental result again accords with this deduction.

iii

LATENT AND IRRELEVANT INCENTIVE LEARNING

The controversy in this field has hinged on whether animals can learn without reward. Though much interesting experimentation has been done in order to test Hull's theory, this theory has not been controverted because reward is a word which has shown itself capable of redefinition. The really interesting question which these experiments have studied, almost without its being noticed, is under what conditions animals can utilize information with which they have been previously confronted. It seems remarkable that animals can use information acquired in no particular order in such a way as to select only the relevant pieces when they are later motivated. It is equally remarkable that they seem incapable of doing this under other circumstances where the problem appears much simpler. It is because of this aspect of the problem that the writer has chosen to treat this topic in a chapter together with reasoning, rather than in the chapter on reward.

It should be clear from the preceding analysis that the hypothesis should explain Blodgett-type latent learning. Here the rat is allowed to explore a maze without a reward. It is then rewarded in one place in the maze and then inserted in it at a different point. The rat can then apparently find its way to the place of reward, perhaps without an error. (This description fits Maier's experiments more closely than does Hull's "conventionalised version.")

The rat, according to the hypothesis, should in its random explorations record the order in which cues occurred. Some of the cues would be noticed again on subsequent explorations. When the animal is motivated and given a reward in the proximity of a distinctive cue, the excitation due to this motivation will flow through a common link to any other rows of links to which it is attached and from these to any further rows of links through links which they have in common. The animal will then find its way to the reward from any

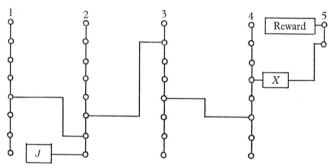

Fig. 17.—The system under conditions of latent learning

point in the maze provided that the cues which it picks up where it is placed are represented by analyzers connected to links which are indirectly influenced by excitation emanating from the link to which the reward analyzer is attached. This may be shown by Figure 17. Suppose that excitation is being introduced at X from row 5. All the rows 1, 2, 3, and 4 will be excited. Also suppose that the animal is so placed in the maze that it is receiving stimulation from an analyzer attached at J. The analyzer attached to the next link on row 2 should soon fire, switching off the excitation both to the link to which J is attached and to row 1. When, while approximating itself to the cue which had set off this analyzer, it picks up signals from the next, row 2 will also be switched off, as will also the initial part of row 3. Further approximation to cues represented by analyzers attached to links still excited can only bring the animal nearer the source of excitation, and so to the reward. The mechanism would operate in the same favorable way if the animal were placed at X with J as the goal. If excitation is introduced into a row via two different links and this gives rise to conflict, it will be resolved by the operation of rules 12 and 13.

From the foregoing it would appear that the animal should find its way to any reward which it noticed, whatever its motivational state. This, however, is a superficial deduction. Though the information may in fact have been registered, it may not in some situations lead toward a correct performance. For instance, many experiments are done in such a way that a prominent identical cue is found in both goal boxes between which the animal must choose on the critical trial (Kendler and Mencher; Grice). An animal is made thirsty and

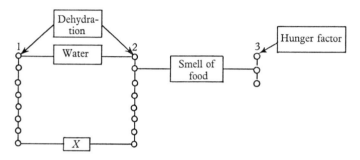

FIG. 18.—The system in Kendler and Mencher's experiment

then run to two goal boxes containing water. In one of these food is also placed. Then the animal is made hungry. It fails to choose the relevant side. Figure 18 shows a schematic representation of the hypothetical mechanism in the animal at the time of the choice in the critical trial. Excitation originating in row *3* owing to hunger is conveyed to row *2* by the common link. Row *2* is excited and this excitation transferred to row *1* via the analyzer common to rows *1* and *2*. As there has been an equal amount of reward and practice on rows *1* and *2*, the only thing which could decide that row *2* should control output is the slight disparity in the number of links through which the excitation has to travel in rows *1* and *2*. It is assumed that such a difference is too small to eventuate in the correct performance.

Such an explanation of the failure to find latent learning in the above situation may not seem plausible. But it can be checked in one or two ways. For instance, if the food link was inserted in the row farther from the beginning of row *2* (farther from the water link) there would be a greater disparity between the number of links between analyzer X on row *1* and row *2*, with the balance more heavily in favor of row *2*. Such experiments (with food as the irrelevant incentive) have in fact been done, one by Thistlethwaite and the other by McAllister with the result deducible from the present theory. They found that rats showed a significant tendency to choose the relevant side when they were made hungry if the relevant reward (water) was widely separated from the irrelevant reward (food) in one of the arms of the maze.

There is another way of testing the hypothesis in its application to the present instance. That is to have two differing relevant incentives in the two arms of the maze with the irrelevant incentive associated with only one. There would thus be no common link to transmit excitation from row *2* to row *1*, in the way the food link does in the diagram. The animal should then make the correct choice. The argument in the above deductions rests on the assumption that there is only a relatively small number of other common links, which are relatively "unique" in the two arms of the maze past the choice point (except those associated with the reward in some instances). Obviously, the greater the number of common features in the two alleys, the less likely the animal is to choose the relevant path. Hence the animal's success will depend on where in the sequence it picked up similar cues (which is usually left to chance, but which could be varied) and on the dissimilarity between the two alternative paths.

Another type of experiment where animals have failed to show any evidence of latent learning is where the relevant reward is placed in one goal box and the irrelevant reward in another (Spence and Lippitt; Kendler). If the animal is repeatedly made hungry and shown water in one alley and then rewarded with food in the other, it will still tend to go toward the food side when it is made thirsty. Assuming there are some similar cues common to both alleys, a portion of the "thirst" excitation arriving at the row of links representing the alley leading to the incentive originally used as reward will be transmitted by a set of links with much lower thresholds. For according to rule 12, the combination of high excitation and reward in this row should have reduced the "resistance" to the passage of excitation considerably in this row. Thus, though it receives less excitation to begin with, any excitation passed on by it should receive less "attenuation." Hence the animal should either behave randomly, fail, or succeed according to the intensity of motivation on the rewarded food trials, the number of times it was food-rewarded and the similarity of cues on either side. Increasing the water motivation on the critical trial should make no difference to its choice. If there had been an equal (or zero) amount of reward on both sides, the animal should choose correctly unless there were strongly similar cues along the two different paths (Kendler; Meehl and MacCorquordale). Strong irrelevant motivation should not in itself hamper the subsequent utilization of information, provided the motivation has not been rewarded. This deduction is borne out by experiments by Walker (1951), by Norton and Kenshalo, and by Strange's (1950) work. Strange used animals which had been deprived of water for 22 hours and gave them an equated amount of training to two goal boxes in a U-maze. One goal box was empty; the other contained food. When the rats were made hungry and allowed to choose, they gave evidence of having learned the location of the food.

In case it is felt that the hypothesis presented is entirely a posteriori, here is a rather curious prediction. Assume there are two rows, both equated for "resistance." Further assume that they both share a link X, but that this link is in different ordinal positions in each. Then if we excite both rows simultaneously and equally, the animal, being given a free choice, should choose the path which contained the cue corresponding to analyzer X nearer to the choice point, though invisible from it. Such an experiment could be performed in the same sort of conditions as a spontaneous alternation experiment.

The hypothesis put forward is, however, exposed to numerous objections. It will be said that it would predict no learning in a situation where the animal has to take a different path to the same goal box according to its motivational condition (though learning to go to different goal boxes should be rapid). That animals find the second easy and the first inordinately difficult does seem to be the case if we examine some experiments which were done to answer a different problem and the interpretation of which has not been clear.

iv

THE HULL-LEEPER EXPERIMENTS

These experiments were performed by Hull (1933) and Leeper (1935) to test whether rats can be taught to make different responses in a constant external situation as a result of changes in their motivation only.

There is a large disagreement between Hull's findings and Leeper's. Hull reports that, giving five trials a day, the rats attained only a 77 per cent accuracy in the first 200 days of training, taking the first trial of the day. On the other hand, Leeper found that his animals attained an accuracy of over 90 per cent on the first trials at the end of only 18 days with five trials a day.

Such a divergence needs to be explained. In both experiments the animals had to learn to turn one way when hungry and another when they were thirsty. To quote Leeper (1935):

> These experiments involved exactly the same procedure and apparatus except that in experiment IIIC there was a double end-box and on an incorrect run the rat could enter the wrong end box and see the undesired goal material in it before it retraced its steps to the correct arm of the maze, whereas in Hull's experiment and in Experiment IIIA, when a rat ran incorrectly its steps led it to a closed door which barred its way into the one end-box and the rat had to retrace its steps as though out of a simple cul-de-sac. . . .

In Hull's experiment, and in Leeper's Experiment IIIA, which is a replication of Hull's, one goal box contained both reward substances, but alternately. It contained only water when the animal was thirsty and only food when it was hungry. In addition, if the animal made the wrong turn, it would go up an alley which had been open when it was in one motivational condition but was now closed because it was in the other motivational condition. In Leeper's own experimental design (IIIC), there were two separate end boxes which the animal was always allowed to reach, each with its specific reward. Leeper attempts to explain the discrepancy in the following way:

> Now to a hungry rat it is probably no greater punishment to be turned back by a door (as in Experiment IIIA) than to be turned back by an end-box containing only a pan of water. Nevertheless this one difference in the situa-

tion seems to make an enormous difference to the rate of mastery of the problem. It would seem, therefore, that the rats must learn almost as much from their incorrect responses as they do from their correct responses.

This conclusion has been widely quoted and accepted by authorities such as Munn (1950). Leeper himself, in another part of the same paper, rather inconsistently favors an alternative explanation which rests on the separateness of the goal boxes in his experiment. He does, in fact, notice that there are at least two differences between his situation and Hull's. In Leeper's situation, there were two goal boxes, and in Hull's only one.

It is possible on the evidence that either or both of the explanations advanced by Leeper are right, but a further experiment is necessary to decide. As the present theory would have predicted the discrepancy noted between the two experiments and further attributed it to the effects of the goal box, and not, in this particular situation, to experience with the irrelevant reward, an experiment was devised by the author. A full account of this has been presented elsewhere (Deutsch, 1959). In this experiment three groups of rats were used. One group was set to learn the maze under Hull's conditions. That is, it was made hungry on one day and thirsty on the next. When the animal was thirsty, only water was placed in the goal box, and the animal would find a block if it ran to the side which was correct when it was hungry. The opposite, but analogous, procedure was adopted when the animal was hungry. The second group was run according to Leeper's design. The food and water were placed in separate goal boxes, and no blocks were ever interposed. The third group was peculiar to this experiment, and the animals in this had only one goal box (as in Hull's experiment). On the other hand, they could obtain experience of the irrelevant reward when they turned the way inappropriate to their motivation. If an animal turned, say, left, it was presented with water when it reached the goal box. If it turned right, it was given food in the same goal box. In this way the animal would be presented with the relevant or irrelevant reward on each trial (relevant to its need, that is). Both the rewards thus appeared in the same goal box, though never at the same time. In this way, the separate effects of sameness of goal box and the presentation of the irrelevant reward could be ascertained. It will be seen that the results of this experiment are very important for the present theory, testing as they do

[119]

the notion of path selection through units nearer the source of motivational excitation.

From the results it appears that it is the same goal box for both rewards which is the factor responsible for retarding learning, because the Hull group and the author's group did not differ significantly in their overall scores (315 as against 313 correct runs), whereas the Leeper group were very much better (387 correct runs). These scores are the totals of each day's runs. So that if we use this criterion of learning, it does *not* appear that "the rats must learn almost as much from their incorrect responses as they do from their correct responses" (Leeper, 1935). In fact, in the present situation they learn nothing at all from seeing the reward when it is irrelevant. It has been shown in other experiments that they can learn from seeing an irrelevant reward, but it will be shown below why, on the present theory, we should not observe such learning in this situation. However, if we take a different criterion of learning, seeing the reward when it is irrelevant does have a beneficial effect. The scores for the first run of the day show that the Leeper group scored 96 trials correct out of 112. The Hull group scores 62, but the group which saw the irrelevant reward in the same goal box scores 72. Here we have a disagreement between two criteria of learning. The temptation is to ask, Which criterion is the "better"? Which should we accept? But such a question should not be asked; it is a misguided question. Both sets of scores are a part of the same picture; each depicts different parts of the same face. They are not competing portraits. Both the scores represent connected facets of the animal's behavior, and they must both be taken into consideration. Of course we cannot take such a view if we conceive our task as mensuration of learning, but this only exposes the futility of any such program.

There are other parts of this picture of behavior which will further serve to emphasize the difficulty of thinking about the differences between the groups in this experiment in terms of overall learning rate. For instance, there is a differential rate of error repetition between the Hull group and the third group in this experiment. If we take the cases where errors could be repeated during a set of daily runs, we find that the Hull group repeats an error in only 9 per cent of the cases. The third group repeats at the rate of 33 per cent, with the difference being highly significant. Meeting a block in an alley does seem to have a highly discouraging effect on the future choice

[120]

of that alley. One of the consequences of this is that there is a difference in the slope of improvement in the daily blocks of trials between the Hull and the third group. The improvement as measured by the difference between correct runs of the first trial and fourth trial of the day is very large. The Hull group improves by almost 50 per cent; the third group, by about 15 per cent. One of the other effects of this discouragement by a block is the difference between the first trial scores of the Hull group and the third group. If the discouragement lasts until the next day, the Hull group should be discouraged by a memory of the block in the path which was incorrect and so blocked on the day before. (It will be recalled that hungry days alternated with thirsty days.) Hence they should be biased toward the path which is now incorrect. However, this incorrect choice should not be repeated, as the block has a strong effect. Obviously, we cannot persist in thinking merely in terms of speeds of learning in the face of such a complicated picture. The problem is to account for the differences observed.

The first and most striking difference is between the Leeper group and the two others in the number of correct runs. The Leeper group, with the two separate goal boxes, showed a striking superiority. Such a difference is to be predicted from the present theory. For the Leeper group, as there are no common points in the maze past the choice-point, two rows of links will be formed with no links in common. Hence, when the animal finds itself at the choice-point, separately motivated for, say, water, the excitation from the thirst link will be conveyed only through one of the rows of links to the link underlying one of the cues at the choice-point between which the animal must choose. Only one set of subgoals past the choice-point will be attractive and it can easily be seen that this will be the correct set.

But suppose that there is a link in common to both rows of links, nearer the sources of excitation than the links underlying the choice-point. This common link will transmit any excitation which reaches it from either the hunger source or the thirst source to both rows of links. Hence, the excitation which would have rendered only one of the cues at the choice-point attractive without this common link, now acts impartially on both alternatives. In this way, both sets of subgoals will become attractive.

In this way, even though a registration of the external sequence of events will have taken place in the nervous system, it will not eventuate in correct performance. And this is to some extent a difficulty for the theory. Some learning does appear in this situation. This would not be expected if the excitation was being distributed equally to both rows of links through the common link. However, it is possible (and this can be tested) that not all the excitation is passing from one row of links to the other. In the present situation only some of the cues from the same goal box need have been common. Owing to the construction of the maze (see Deutsch, 1959) the animal could see the goal box from a different angle, depending on whether it was entering it from the left or the right. In this way, some of the links in parallel at this point would not be common to both rows. This would enable the two series of links to be differentially excited, even though this differentiation might be slight and mistakes therefore frequent.

With repeated reward the attenuation of the excitation by the row of links would gradually diminish and mistakes gradually decrease as the absolute differences between the excitations arriving at the links underlying the cues at the choice-point increased. On this view the ability of rats to learn in the one goal-box situation should disappear if they are forced to enter the goal box in the same way whichever choice they have made. This could be secured, for example, by a lengthening of the alley joining the two paths to the goal box.

A further point which we can explain if we assume that the motivational excitation from hunger and thirst was being distributed to a large extent to both rows of links is the apparent lack of benefit to the third group from the sight of the irrelevant incentive. It has been shown by other experiments, such as those of Spence, Bergmann, and Lippitt (1950), that experience of an irrelevant reward does lead to learning. But in their experiment the two rows of links formed would not have common links nearer the sources of excitation than the choice-point. In the present situation the animals in the third group were presented with the irrelevant incentives after they had seen the common goal box. That is, any lowering of the threshold of the appropriate link would simply have an effect on excitation which is distributed to both rows through the common links. Therefore, the present situation would be a bad one for showing the effects on learning of irrelevant reward.

So far it has been suggested why there should be a difference between the groups with two goal boxes and those with only one, and why the sight of an irrelevant incentive in this situation should not affect performance to any significant extent. It remains now to explain the differences in sequential dependencies between the Hull and the third group. This may be done as follows. Supposing that an animal in the Hull group makes a mistake and comes up against a block (see Fig. 19). Then one of the links in this row will become more resistant to the passage of excitation (as the normal sequence of subgoals has not occurred). As this break in the normal sequence of subgoals occurs between the common cue and the choice-point, the flow of excitation is lessened to the link, underlying the cue which has just been chosen at the choice-point. Therefore if an animal encounters a block in the alley, it will be much less likely to

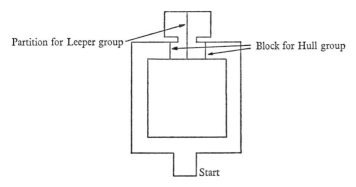

FIG. 19.—Schematic diagram of "Hull-Leeper" maze

repeat its error than the animal in the third group. Here there is no break in the sequence of cues, and, therefore, the relative probability of one wrong response occurring after another remains high. By the same token the rate of "learning" within a day's block of trials will be much smaller for the third group than for the Hull group. Also, the number of correct trials, if we take those occurring first on each day after a change in motivation, will be higher in the third group than for the Hull group. For the Hull group, the break in the sequence of the cues due to the block in the alley, which was incorrect before motivation was changed, will still have some attenuating effect on the excitation being transmitted down that row of links. It is therefore predicted that with longer intervals between the blocks of trials a greater number of the first trials after a change in motivation will become correct for the Hull group.

[123]

X

A Mechanical Interpretation

In the foregoing chapters a theoretical system was put forward to account for some of the behavior of a rat. To show that the theory was really the description of a mechanism in general terms and not a set of neologisms redescribing behavior, a machine was built embodying the system. A somewhat simplified version of the system was adopted as it proved possible to reproduce those main features of behavior where prediction in the abstract could have been most fallible.

The machine consists of three main parts. The first is a small trolley running on two wheels and a ball bearing. The trolley is square in shape, with three bumpers protecting the front and sides. When the front bumper is touched, the trolley turns, always in one direction. When one of the bumpers on the side is touched, the wheel on the opposite side goes into reverse and the trolley steers away from the obstacle with which it had come into contact. The two wheels, one on each side of the trolley, are separately driven by two motors. One of these motors is reversed not only when the bumper on the opposite side is touched but also when the trolley receives a pulse through the remote-control circuit from the central part of the machine. While this pulse continues, the trolley turns. When it stops, both the motors turn in the same direction again, and so the trolley goes forward.

Besides the motors and the bumpers the trolley carries some batteries, a remote-control transistor circuit, designed by P. G. M. Dawe, and a bulb. This bulb has a reflector behind it in such a way that a cone of light is thrown forward.

The second part of the machine consists of a rat maze with photo-cells mounted at various points on the walls. The photocells are connected to the central part of the machine whenever the light from the trolley falls on them. The photocells fulfil the same function as receptors in an animal. Their unorthodox position does not prevent them from exercising the same function as their analogues in the animal. When the beam on the trolley stimulates a photocell, the position of the trolley is indicated to the central part of the machine in much the same way as when an animal sees a landmark and fixes its own whereabouts by it.

The third and central part of the machine is made of relays and uniselectors and may be compared in its function to the central nervous system. Each of the photocells in the maze is connected to a specific place in this system. From it the pulse controlling the turning of the trolley is sent out. Here are also situated the two switches which determine which of two goals open to it the machine seeks.

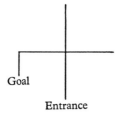

FIG. 20.—A schematic diagram of the maze used for the machine

After the machine's performance, the construction of the machine will be described.

It is possible for the machine to learn a simple maze (Fig. 20). On the first run when the machine is placed at the start it is made to enter each blind alley in turn. This is done by blocking off the various sections of the maze first to prevent entry and then to prevent re-entry. (Such a procedure saves the experimenter's time, as do analogous procedures in animal-training. The trolley is prevented from blundering about at random. Also a repeated stimulation of the photocells would necessitate a larger "storage capacity" in the machine.) The machine is in this way forced through the whole maze until it reaches the goal. The goal is simply a photocell attached to a certain section of the central system.

Now that the goal has been found, the trolley can be inserted again at the entrance. A switch is turned which "motivates" the machine to seek the goal, and all the blocks are extracted from the maze. The machine now advances to the choice-point,

[125]

perhaps bumping into the walls of the maze as it goes. At the choice-point it turns down the alley leading to the goal without entering either of the two blind alleys.

The machine, having learned the maze, can now take advantage of a short cut without any further learning (Fig. 21). Suppose that an alley is inserted as in the figure so that a point nearer the goal than the choice-point can be "seen" from the entrance. The machine will proceed down this new alley immediately this alley has been inserted.

The machine's learning and performance are independent of its precise movements. The machine can learn to run the maze without error even if it is making no "motor response" (that

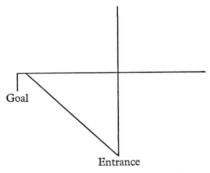

Goal

Entrance

FIG. 21.—The maze with a short cut inserted

is, if the trolley is not running). The trolley can just be picked up and taken round the maze by the experimenter. All that is necessary for learning is the stimulation of the machine's receptors. An experiment of this sort on the rat originally suggested by Thorndike (1946) has been recently successfully performed by Gleitman (1955) and by McNamara, Long, and Wike (1956) to the great embarrassment of the Hullians and Pavlovian learning theorists.

The machine after it has learned does not execute the same set of movements on any two trials. The path traversed always differs, even though no errors as measured by blind-alley entrances occur. It is even possible to lift the trolley out of the maze and place it back in the alley facing the other way round without affecting the overall correctness of its performance. It has happened that one of the wheels on the trolley was imperfectly fitted to its axle, with the result that the machine tended to circle. Even under this condition of being partially crippled the machine executed an error-less run.

The machine can transfer or generalize its "knowledge" to mazes of completely different shape and similar only in a highly abstract way. Each alley in the maze is marked by a different photocell which signals to the central part of the machine. If the sequential order of the signals shown in the alleys is kept the same (as in mazes *A* and *B*, Fig. 22), even though the shape of the maze is quite altered, the machine can still find its way. It will execute an errorless run even though it may now have to turn in opposite directions at the choice-points. The machine does not learn a sequence of responses to a chain of appropriate stimuli.

The machine is capable of "reasoning" or "insight." After the machine has learned one maze, it can learn another one which

Fig. 22.—Three different mazes used in the experiment. The machine transfers its training from *A* to *B* and vice versa, but not from *A* to *C*.

it can "remember" concomitantly. If the second one has a landmark (photocell) in common with the first, we can set it the following problem (Fig. 23).We place it at the entrance of maze *1* from which it has learned to find its way to goal *1* on a previous occasion. The block which separated maze *1* from maze *2* is removed. Instead of setting it the task of finding goal *1* as previously, we can give it the problem of finding goal *2* in the other maze. It has never in fact been from maze *1* to maze *2* (or vice versa), as the way was blocked. Nevertheless the machine solves the problem. At the choice-point in maze *1* it turns into what was previously a blind alley and approaches the common landmark. After this it runs toward goal *2* without error. This type of problem solution would be called "reasoning" or "insight" if it were observed in an animal.

Other properties, such as goal-seeking and motivation, are to some extent imitated. Thus the machine, when it is set in a maze where it always previously turned to the right to go to one goal,

[127]

will turn to the left when it has been set another goal. The response is not merely a function of the "peripheral stimulation" at the moment but also of the "motivation."

i

THE SYSTEM IN THE MACHINE

The behavior described above is the behavior of a certain type of system. The properties described are not those of relays but of

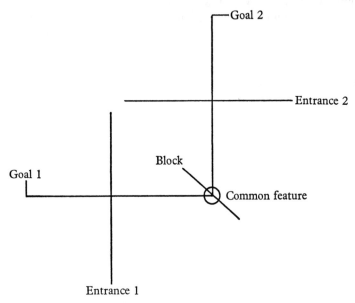

FIG. 23.—The double maze with block in place

arrangements of relays. Further, we can make the same arrangement, manifesting the same behavior, out of other components—electron tubes, transistors, or wheels. Perhaps a similar arrangement is to be found in the mammalian central nervous system. After all, the mammal manifests similar behavior.

The abstract system itself, which is richer, is described in a previous chapter. Here are described the operations which the machine performs and its particular embodiment as represented by this machine.

On the learning trial (before the goal is found) the system arranges the receptors in an order inverse to that in which they were stimulated. The receptor which was set off first will be last in the series, and the last one next to the first. The first position is always occupied by the goal-signaling receptor. There will therefore be a record of the order in which certain aspects of the environment occur in relation to the goal.

This order is preserved by making a pulse from a receptor travel to the trolley through a contact on relay with what might be called a particular number. The relay with the lowest number has the goal-signaling receptor already attached to it, and when it is switched on and closed by the operator, all the relays with higher numbers are closed, enabling any receptor attached to any of them to control the trolley, whichever it is that may be stimulated.

But when a pulse passes through any relay, all those relays which have a higher number will open and stay open so that the receptors attached to them will not be able to influence the movements of the trolley. This will be called the hierarchical arrangement. It insures that the trolley will always steer toward that "landmark" which it "saw" nearest (in time) to the goal.

When there are two series of receptors made, each registering the order of "cues" leading to the two goals, if there is a receptor common to both series, the system will exploit this information. When one of the goal-signal receptors is closed by the operator, it will be recalled that all the relays with higher numbers will also be switched on. Now one of the relays with a higher number has a receptor common to both series attached to it; through this common receptor will now flow excitation closing all the relays in the other series with a higher number. This gives the system "insight."

ii

THE MACHINE

The system is embodied in the following way. First is the "thinking" part, composed of six uniselectors and twenty-three relays. The second is the trolley which moves through the maze, and the third consists of the photocell receptors. The trolley has a light mounted on it, which is thrown forward at a wide angle, and which touches off the photocells mounted on each sector of the maze. (This arrangement was adopted as a practically easier equivalent of mounting receptors on the trolley and placing the signals in the maze.) The trolley has two responses: it either goes forward or turns round on its axis. When it has been set to learn its way to a goal, it goes forward (except when it bumps into the walls of the maze). When it has been set to find its way after it has learned, it will continue to travel forward as long as a particular receptor which the machine has selected is being stimulated. When this stimulation ceases, the machine will turn until the stimulation of this receptor occurs again.

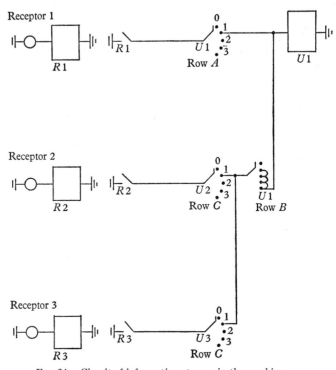

Fig. 24.—Circuit of information storage in the machine

It will thus guide itself toward the selected receptor. This is the way in which the trolley is controlled.

The way in which the machine stores the order in which the receptors were stimulated on the learning trial is now described (see Fig. 24).

Each receptor is connected to its uniselector before it has been stimulated, in such a way that its stimulation will move the wipers of its own uniselector to the first position and the wipers of any other uniselector whose receptor has already been stimulated to the next position. Once it has been stimulated and the wipers shifted to the first position, the stimulation from its own receptor will not affect the connected uniselector; nor will it affect any other uniselector. It will now only be shifted by a receptor which is being stimulated for the first time.

This will be made clear if we study Figure 24. The uniselector *U1*, which is moved when receptor *1* is stimulated, has two principal states:

1. The state before receptor *1* has been stimulated. Here only the closing of relay *R1*, caused by the stimulation of receptor *1*, will move the wipers of *U1* from position *0*. Any pulse from *R2*, closed by the stimulation of receptor *2*, will not affect *U1* because the circuit which effects this is broken at *U1*, row *B*.

2. The state after receptor *1* has been stimulated. Here the closing of *R1* will not further affect *U1*, because the wipers have now been shifted to position *1*. And thus the circuit which shifts *U1* when *R1* closes will have been broken.

On the other hand, the circuit which connects *U1* with *R2* and *R3* is now closed by *U1*, row *B; U1* will therefore be stepped on when *R2* or *R3* closes. But *U1* will be affected only if *R2* (or *R3*) closes for the first time because the circuit leading through *U2* row *C* (or *U3*, row *C*) will be broken as soon as the wipers have been moved from position *0*.

When considering receptor *n*, substitute *n* for *1* in the above description and vice versa.

Now, if there are three receptors stimulated in turn, it follows that the uniselector attached to the first one to be stimulated will be on the third position, the next on the second position, and the last on the first position.

The receptors are also connected through wipers on another row of their uniselectors to the positions, each of which is separately attached to the hierarchical arrangement. Thus, the nearer in time to the goal a receptor was touched off, the higher in the hierarchy is it connected. Once the goal the machine was set to discover is found, the connection becomes permanent. As on the learning run the trolley is made to "explore" each alley or sector in turn before it reaches the goal, the receptors are connected to the hierarchical arrangement in accordance with their proximity to the goal receptor.

[131]

The order thus preserved is utilized in the following manner (see Fig. 25).

The receptors are connected by uniselectors to a hierarchical arrangement of relays. By this is meant that the relays are connected in a series in which the energizing of a preceding (supraordinate) relay causes the closing of its successor (subordinate), and the switching-off of a predecessor leads to the opening of the relay whose closing it previously caused.

The receptor whose stimulation functions as goal (two in the present model) is "innately" connected to the "make" contacts of the first relay in this series (RA) (again two in the present model) (see Fig. 25). The rest of the receptors (X, Y) are also connected

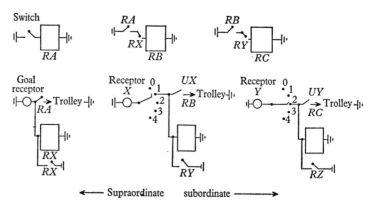

FIG. 25.—Circuit of hierarchical arrangement

to the make contacts of relays, but each is connected to its respective relay in the hierarchy through the activity of its uniselector (UX, UY) during the "training" trial. Each receptor is connected at the same time to close another relay (RX, RY, RZ) which breaks the circuit of the relay subordinate to the one to which the receptor is also connected by the uniselector. When the hierarchy is switched on ("when there is a drive acting on the organism"), the stimulation of any receptor connected to the hierarchy will cause the trolley to go forward while this stimulation continues, because it is connected to the trolley through the make contact on its relay in the hierarchy and, second, will immediately lead to the opening, for the rest of the trial, of all the relays subordinate to that to which it is connected.

During the training trial the hierarchy is not switched on. Instead

[132]

the circuit which allows the receptors to drive the uniselectors is closed, to be opened when the finding of the goal receptor is signaled.

On being set in the entrance of the maze on the test trial, the machine is set to find the goal. The hierarchical arrangement of relays is now switched on and some receptors again pick up signals.

As has been explained, the receptors when they are stimulated send a pulse to the trolley through that portion of the hierarchy to which they are attached, but only when this portion is switched on at the same time. A portion is switched off as soon as another portion supraordinate to its has passed a pulse from the receptor, attached to it, to the trolley. Hence the trolley will always steer toward the receptor nearest to the goal and bring itself by this means within the range of stimulation of others even nearer until it reaches the goal receptor.

When the trolley has learned two mazes with a common receptor and two separate goals, the one receptor is attached to both hierarchies perhaps with a different position in each. When either goal is then selected, the switching-on of the hierarchy subordinate to that goal will be transmitted through the common receptor to portions of the other hierarchy. Only those portions subordinate to that to which this common receptor is connected will be switched on. Hence the trolley will find the shortest way to the goal selected in whichever entrance it is set.

The system consists of six uniselectors and twenty-three relays. The uniselectors have six wipers each, and are ordinary P.O. equipment. Only three positions are employed on each. Smaller ones would thus be more suitable, were they obtainable. The relays are similarly large P.O. relays with four "make" and one "break" contact. These also are often not all used, but the writer, and constructor, was led to use them because they were cheap and readily available and because he believes that he would have become intolerably confused had he used more than one type.

The system is such that it could be expanded without a loss in efficiency. For instance, even the time taken to calculate a choice or reach a decision does not vary with the complexity of the operation (and the size of the system); it takes the machine no longer to select the path to a goal whether it has to combine information acquired in separate situations or not. This, with the number of complex properties which this relatively simple system has in common with a mammalian organism, is encouraging from the point of view of theoretical psychology.

[133]

XI

Some Perceptual Mechanisms

i

INTRODUCTION

The purpose of this chapter is twofold. First, it is intended to show by another practical example the fruitfulness of a view of psychological theory put forward in the first chapter. There it was argued that the task of a theory in psychology is to infer the system or mechanism which is producing the phenomena of behavior without necessarily giving the embodiment of such a system. That such a policy was practically feasible at this stage was shown by the construction of a system whose properties tallied closely with those of a motivated learning organism. Further, to show that this theory was really the description of a mechanism in general terms and not a redescription of the behavior of an animal in highfalutin language, a machine was actually built embodying this system. It is intended here to give another example of such a theory and to show how this approach is of use in the study of perception.

The second object is partially to fill what many felt to be a gap in the previous theory. The system described in the preceding chapters dealt with and acted on information which had already been digested. The process of classifying environmental stimulation was taken for granted.

A theory of shape recognition.—In this section an attempt is made to elaborate a mechanism of shape perception which is complementary to the behavior system. Though there have been previous attempts in this direction, none of the models suggested has had properties which tallied sufficiently with the known peculiarities of shape recognition in animals. Nor was it possible to put them to test, as they made no particular further prediction about behavior.

Accordingly, they have more the status of inventions than of explanatory theories.

ii

What are these known peculiarities which any theory concerning the subject must explain? There are six main facts:

a) Animals can recognize shapes independent of their location in the visual field. It is not necessary to fixate the center of a figure in order to recognize it nor need the eyes be moved around the contours of a figure.

b) Recognition can be effected independently of the angle of inclination of a figure in the visual field. (By this is not meant tilt of the figure in depth, such as occurs in shape constancy experiments, but the tilt of an image in its own plane.)

c) The size of a figure does not interfere with the identity of its shape. This of course does not hold at the extremes of size, for reasons which seem sufficiently obvious.

d) Mirror images appear alike. Both rats and human beings tend to confuse these. This would tend to rule out any "template" theories of shape recognition. According to these a contour is rotated in two dimensions until it coincides with one of the many patterns already laid down. But such a superimposition cannot take place in the case of mirror images and no room is left for this particular type of confusion.

e) Visually primitive organisms such as the rat find it hard (perhaps impossible) to distinguish between squares and circles. This does not seem to be a limitation imposed by the peripheral characteristics of the optical system. It appears to be a more central defect, as these organisms can distinguish shapes which are far more alike geometrically. This type of evidence tends to cast doubt on theories which base themselves on the angular properties of figures. To quote Lashley (1938): "The pair of figures giving greatest difficulty of discrimination where the element of acuity might play a part are the square and the circle. In several experiments these have required from 60 to 300 trials for learning and only one-fourth of the animals have shown any improvement above chance. Yet acuity is certainly not the chief limiting factor in this case."

f) These abilities, which appear to be mediated by the striate cortex, survive the removal of the major part of it. It is, therefore,

[135]

unreasonable to suppose that this ability to disentangle shape is common to all parts of the striate area and that one part of the striate area is not essential in helping the next one to operate.

This consideration would tend to rule out notions based on a scanning process. It is difficult to see how a regular scan could be maintained in the presence of extensive damage. Further, any system which requires the fixation of the center of a figure so that it coincides with the center of the visual field must also be ruled out. The ability is maintained even when there are extensive scotomata of central origin.

In what follows, a system is proposed which will abstract form and yet satisfy the above specifications. It will also lead to fresh predictions about the discriminability of certain figures. It is therefore testable.

It is not suggested that it is the only system concerned in recognition. There must be other systems devoted to the recognition of brightness, location, and size. This makes many experiments on pattern discrimination difficult to assess from the point of view of evidence for the mechanism of shape discrimination pure and simple. Some support for the notion that there are separate mechanisms is given by a conclusion of Poppelreuter, reported by Klüver.

> Poppelreuter arrives "inductively" on the basis of some hundred cases, at "principles" of dissolution as regards the visual system in cerebral lesions. According to him, we have to do, firstly, with a number of part systems: (1) the brightness systems; (2) the colour system; (3) the form system; (4) movement; (5) direction. These different part systems may be more or less independently disturbed [Klüver, 1927, p. 342].

iii

THE SYSTEM

Let us assume that there is an array of units (or cells) arranged in two dimensions, each unit having many neighbors. This plane composed of cells has messages arriving on it from light receptors (or the retina). Each group of cells is joined to a particular retinal element in such a way that neighboring retinal elements also excite neighboring groups of cells on this two-dimensional array. But it is assumed that only a particular source of excitation is passed on from the retina. This is excitation from contours, the regions of the sharpest change.

Thus when a ball is focused on the retina the contour of this ball is projected on this two-dimensional array. Excitation in the form of a circle will appear on it. Thus we have the first rule.

1. Each unit on the two-dimensional array can be excited by a contour falling on the region of the retina to which it is joined.

2. When such excitation from the retina arrives, each unit will pass on a pulse down what will be called a final common cable. It will also excite its neighbor. This neighbor will pass it on in its turn. Therefore when a contour is projected on the two-dimensional array, two things will occur: a message consisting of one pulse will be passed down the final common cable by each cell or unit on which that contour lies. Thus a measure of the total number of cells stimulated will be passed down.

3. The contour will also excite all the cells which lie next to it on the two-dimensional array. These will pass the excitation on to their neighbors but not down the final common cable. The assumption is made that a cell will pass on its excitation at right angles to the contour of which it happens to be a component. Thus, for instance, the excitation produced by a straight line will be a line equal and parallel to it and gradually moving away. In the case of a curve, for instance an arc of a circle, it will also be an arc of a circle moving away "parallel" to it, but gradually decreasing as it draws away, coming to a point and then fanning out again, this time reversed (since all the advancing points of excitation move at the same speed from the point of their origin).

4. As such lateral excitation from a point in a contour advances, another message will be sent down the final common cable as soon as it coincides with another point in a contour imposed on the two-dimensional array.

This message down the final common cable will at each moment give a measure of the number of points thus brought into coincidence. For example, if the figure is a rectangle, the first set of pulses sent down the final common cable will be a measure of the total number of cells excited lying on the contour (rules 1 and 2). The second set of pulses down the final common cable will be sent when the excitation traveling in a parallel line (rule 3) coincides with the two longer sides.

As these two sides are parallel to each other, the excitation and the contours will coincide simultaneously and send a number of pulses proportionate to the length of these sides down the final common path, all at the same instant of time. Some time later the disturbance from the two shorter lines will reach each of these lines and another message will be sent down the final common cable, indicating that a smaller number of cells has been fired off this time but also all simultaneously. Thus the message sent down the final common cable from any rectangle will consist of three sharp volleys, the proportions of the last two being governed by the ratio of the longer to the shorter sides. The message generated by a square will be two sharp volleys, both equal in magnitude. As the two pairs of sides are equidistant, the advancing disturbances will hit the sides simultaneously. As they are parallel, the disturbance generated and the contours will overlap all along their length at the same instant of time, causing the cells representing the contour to fire down the final common path together.

Oddly enough, a circle too would generate two sharp volleys, both equal in magnitude. All the pairs of points lying opposite each other are equidistant. Therefore, the disturbance traveling across would reach all the opposite parts of the contour simultaneously—a sharp pulse equal to the first, when the circular contour first arrived on the two-dimensional array. Thus, if we agree that it is the number and relative size of the pulses that are made use of at the next stage in primitive organisms in distinguishing shapes, then circles and squares will be treated as identical. (But this may be due to the poor acuity of the sorting mechanism [see below].) Thus the theory so far would predict the fifth finding (fact *e*) about the confusion between squares and circles. There is another group of predictions which appears prima facie unlikely and which has not been tested. This is that a pentagon and all odd-sided regular polygons, until there is a breakdown of acuity (central and peripheral), ought to be discriminable from a circle by these organisms where a square, a hexagon, etc., would not be.

To make the logic of this deduction clear, let us consider an equilateral triangle, the simplest of the regular polygons without parallel sides. As soon as this is projected on the two-dimensional array, a message will be sent down the final common cable giving a measure of the total length of the contour. Immediately after this the three sides will propagate lines of disturbance parallel to themselves. As these lines of disturbance meet the contours of the triangle, there

[138]

will be another message sent down the final common cable. But this time the cells on the contour will not fire off all together, as the disturbance will pass across them obliquely. Their firing will be staggered according to the angle at which the disturbance and the contour interact. Thus, in the case of the equilateral triangle, there will be a large initial spike or sharp volley followed immediately by a much smaller continuous discharge, which will suddenly cease.

In the case of the pentagon there will be a large and sudden first spike (as with all figures) followed by a gap (before the disturbances make contact with the opposite sides). There will then be a message of a much smaller magnitude and spread out in time, following it as the disturbance meets the opposite contours obliquely. The pentagon then, given this system of encoding and decoding, ought to be quite easily discriminable from both a circle and a square, while these latter appear the same.

In spite of this interesting confusion it would seem that this system would derive fairly distinctive messages from most shapes which cannot be superimposed. There are two exceptions to this which are again important. This is the case of mirror images (fact *d*), another interesting fact which seems accounted for. The same message will be sent down the final common cable as long as the relations of angle to length of side remain the same internal to the figure.

The second relates to figures with highly complex and irregular contours and internal lines. Unless there is some regularity of geometrical arrangement within complicated figures, the messages down the final common cable generated by these will tend to approximate with growing complexity. There would be a very large initial spike followed by a continuous signal as the many disturbances set up by contours hit other contours continuously. Any feature of equal or parallel spacing, which we normally call regularity, would set up messages which were synchronous and, thus, additive or sharp, giving rise to distinctive peaks in the message. Absence of these would lead to the opposite. This tallies with Lashley's (1938) experimental findings: "The indications are that a somewhat larger number of animals fail to discriminate irregular geometrical figures, but those which do discriminate require no longer to learn the one than the other type. There is evidence that those animals which learn to do so by isolating some simpler cue or part figure."

The system outlined would also display the properties of sending the same message down the final common cable whatever the inclination or position of the figure on the two-dimensional array (facts $a + b$). The message generated depends entirely on the properties of the figure itself, and not on its relation with some external axes.

So far only one fact of the original six is left unexplained. This is the animal's ability to recognize shape independent of size (fact c). It would be possible to reconstitute differences in size from the messages passing down the final common cable generated by various shapes, though it would not be possible to ascertain their position on the two-dimensional array. On the other hand, only certain aspects of the message passing down the final common cable will be determined by the size of the shape. The first is the size of the initial pulse (the occurrence of which is not essential for crude shape-differentiation) and the length in time of the various components of the message. What is unaffected by the size of the shape is the frequency composition of the message which is determined by the angles at which the various lines are to each other, and not their length. The size invariance of shapes would then be expressed by the frequencies they generated as apart from the duration of each frequency burst.

Further refinements in such a system could be envisaged by taking account of the order in which the component frequencies arrived and also the relative durations of their arrival. The relative durations of arrival of the various components of a message would be possible in some such way as follows. If we suppose this is a synaptic arrangement which is rendered refractory by the size of a "setting pulse," this synapse will pass on another pulse if it is in definite temporal relation to the first pulse and its size. As the length of a contour of a shape provides such a setting pulse when the shape first fires, the length of a refractory period in one such synapse will be proportionate to the size of the shape. Whether the next pulse signaling, let us say, a change of frequency, is passed on by this synaptic arrangement will depend on the ratio of the size of the setting pulse (the first pulse generated by the whole contour) to the time between the two pulses. Thus the synaptic arrangement will either fire or not, depending on the ratio of the contour of the shape to the distances within it. We may furthermore suppose that a group of such synaptic arrangements exists and that these are rendered refractory for varying degrees of time by the same sized setting pulse. These would respond or not depending on the ratio of size to time between pulses. Taking the group of such synaptic arrangements as a whole, the number firing would give an estimate of such a ratio. The greater the number covering the range of possible ratios, the better the discrimination of such a system.

So far a mechanism has been suggested to reduce a purely relational entity, a shape regardless of its location, size, and inclination, to a unique set of physical events. This mechanism also shares some other rather peculiar properties with an animal's shape-recognition mechanism. It is therefore supposed that such a mechanism is in fact that used by an animal.

This mechanism has other properties which follow as predictions:

1. It should prove easier to discriminate between a square and a rectangle than between a square and a rectangle both with one side missing.

2. There should be an almost perfect transfer from an equilateral triangle to another with one side missing. This agrees with Lashley's findings, but this type of transfer should be worse in the case of other triangles, where the removal of a side should make a great difference. For instance, the removal of the hypotenuse in the case of a right-angled triangle should militate more strongly against transfer.

3. Shallow curves should be indistinguishable from straight lines in the absence of other contours in the vicinity. (It may be that the factor of a change of direction in the case of the curve may provide a cue here. The same applies to many open contours.)

4. If shallow curves and straight lines are indistinguishable, their addition to otherwise identical figures should make these discriminable. For instance, the substitution of a curved side in a rectangle, should differentiate it from the normal rectangle. This effect should be smaller for most triangles.

5. A "mixture" of a square and a circle should be distinct from these, even though they are not distinct from each other. In fact, transfer to a rectangle ought to be easier in some circumstances, for instance, where two arcs of a circle complete a square with two opposite sides missing.

6. A scotoma of central origin when falling wholly inside a figure, where there are no contours in the vicinity, should prevent identification of the shape.

7. The prediction concerning regular polygons with an odd num-

ber of sides has already been made. It will be noted that all these predictions are independent in the sense that it would be difficult to subsume any two under a single generalization. If, to the writer's greatest surprise, some of these predictions receive experimental confirmation, it may be worth drawing a few more deductions from the theory.

There are, however, some difficulties.

Such a mechanism could handle only one figure at a time. Consider the effect on the message down the final common cable of a square and a triangle in two different parts of the field. The two messages would be inextricably mixed up or superimposed, as they would be sent down at one and the same time. They should therefore mask each other to a certain extent. But they are in fact recognized easily and separately, except in one interesting condition. This is when the contours actually touch or cross. It is, therefore, suggested that figures are passed to the two-dimensional array on the following principle. Assume that the points in the visual field are arranged in an arbitrary order of precedence. The stimulating point which is highest in order will inhibit all the others, preventing their passage until another signal (such as might arise from the final identification apparatus) is sent up. Then the next point in order of precedence will be dealt with. Now consider the case where such points have neighbors. Assume that the effects of this inhibition are overcome by a supervening excitation passed on from this point which is inhibiting all others to those of its neighbors (if any) that were also excited, and passed on by these. (It is assumed that interrupted contours are completed.) In this way a whole contour is passed on (and other contours are kept in "cold storage") until it is dealt with. If this was the case, masking of one figure by another would occur as soon as their outlines touched. They would now be dealt with as one complex figure. Something of the sort is borne out by everyday experience and Gottschaldt's experiment (1926). In any case this is merely to show that this property of being able to handle only one shape at a time can be circumvented by an additional hypothesis.

Higher forms can distinguish squares from circles. There is no evidence that human beings have any difficulty at all in this. It would be more plausible to propose a mechanism which would preserve a phylogenetic continuity. There can be quite a simple "evolutionary" development of this system to work with greater

[142]

precision and to make this distinction. The encoding part of the mechanism can be kept the same and the same message sent down the final common cable. But the message must be sent to a detecting mechanism which has a greater "acuity" in its pulse-sorting mechanism, i.e., if there is a greater number of synaptic mechanisms to cover the range of ratios of pulse height to pulse space. These are fairly close in the case of the square and the circle (4 to 3.14).

A circle's boundary is shorter than that of a square when the distance to be traveled by the laterally spreading disturbance from contour to contour is the same. Therefore, though the two pulses sent down in each case are of the same height, there will be a greater distance between the two pulses even though they are of the same height. Such a possibility of improving the system by simply increasing the number of sorting synaptic mechanisms to cover the same range without any basic change perhaps gives the whole suggestion an enhanced biological plausibility.

It will doubtless be objected that nothing has been done to explain the lateral spread with the convenient properties postulated for it. No *modus operandi* has been suggested. This is admittedly a weakness of the hypothesis, logically speaking. We ought in principle to state what family of machine performs this task, what interrelationships we postulate among our elements. On the other hand, from the point of view of practical science, to suggest possible networks of some complexity merely because they are required theoretically would be somewhat foolish, especially as there is nothing to distinguish between rival possibilities. It is really only necessary to ask whether it is plausible to assign such a property to the nervous system. Has anything like it in fact been found?

Evidence of a laterally spreading process has been found in the visual cortex by Burns (1950, 1951) and Burns and Grafstein (1952) in the cat. Its properties, however, remain incompletely investigated, and it is too early to say how far the postulated process coincides in its properties with this cortical spread. Burns reports in a series of papers how he has succeeded in detaching a small slab of the cat's visual cortex from the rest of the nervous tissue but with blood supply intact. This slab, when the last bridge with the rest of the cortex has been severed, ceases, interestingly enough, to show signs of electrical activity. However, when a stimulating electrode is inserted in this piece of cortex, two distinct phenomena are obtainable. Below a certain stimulus strength, a negative response can be

[143]

picked up from the immediately surrounding tissue. This has a velocity of about 2 m/sec and it appears that in this response no synapses are involved. However, when the stimulus strength increases beyond a certain point, a positive discharge appears, which bears an all-or-none relationship to the stimulus strength. It travels at 10–20 cm/sec and it is possible that it traverses synapses in its progress, as it suffers no attenuation as it travels. Transmission ceases when a cut is made which is roughly $1\frac{1}{4}$ m. deep. It is interesting to note that conduction of this wave is impossible without intact cell connections, especially in regard to Köhler and Wallach's theory. The slow speeds of transmission observed are not due to anesthesia, as sets of experiments were done without general anesthesia. Again too much should not be made of this observation. The precise properties and function of this process remain unknown and such a finding can only be treated as suggestive.

Further evidence of a more detailed nature has been obtained by Lilly and Cherry (1954), who have studied the propagation of waves in the cortex by a more elaborate technique. Unfortunately the results they report are for the acoustic projection areas. However, their observations do at least show what type of operation the cortex is capable of. These workers used a recording technique which gives information about the electrical stimulation received simultaneously by twenty-five electrodes implanted in the cortex. Cats were employed and stimulated by clicks. It is found that a traveling wave appears which moves at a high velocity of about 1 m/sec over the cortex. This is called the "leading edge." This leading edge travels rather more slowly (at a tenth of its speed) past a definite boundary. The leading edge is succeeded by the dying-away of activity which is called the trailing edge, whose speed is in close correspondence with that of the slower leading edge.

Lilly and Cherry (1954, p. 530) believe that

> . . . in the light of the above known and postulated connections for acoustic I and II, the high velocity leading edge is probably due to a preformed afferent figure moving up to cortex from below, firing the cortical cells first anteriorly and then posteriorly. Thus the leading edge reflects sequential firing of cortex by impulses coming into cortex at different times at different places: the "velocity" of the leading edge reflects these differences.

[144]

Now these ascending impulses in a modified form could represent contours being written up quickly on the surface of the cortex. The leading edge would not then be extended but would be a quickly traveling point or narrow edge. If we make this modification, a surprising fact emerges.

> If the charts for the sequential positions of the leading and of the trailing edges are superimposed for each cat separately, it is found that the two sets of iso-latency lines tend to lie at angles to each other nearer 90° than 0° or 180°.... In other words, except in a region showing relatively surface-negative activity, the trailing edge tends to move over the cortex in directions which approach angles close to 90° to the directions taken previously by the leading edge [Lilly and Cherry, 1954, pp. 528–29].

With the modification suggested above the trailing edge then has the property of the propagated wave front suggested in the theory which is postulated to move away at right angles from the contour. Further, the authors believe that the speed of the trailing edge is determined, not by afferent factors but to cell-to-cell firing within the cortex. This again would fit in with the theory.

A more complete neurophysiological verification would be possible with the techniques at present available by observation on the visual cortex. It should be possible to determine, when contours are exhibited to the animal, whether there are waves propagated at right angles to these contours and whether they cross over each other. It might also be possible to establish whether a special excitation occurred when a laterally spreading wave coincided with the place occupied by a contour process. It would also be interesting to find out what the repetition frequency is of the propagation of the laterally spreading waves.

Dodwell and Sutherland have recently put forward theories of shape discrimination in which a pattern is measured against two external co-ordinates, one horizontal and one vertical. They have carried out experiments to show that tilt is an important ingredient in the animal's visual world. Their systems would detect tilt rather than absolute shape. Similarities between figures would tend to be destroyed by rotation. Criticisms have been made (especially by Dodwell) of the writer's theory, because animals can be shown to make discriminations such as those involving tilt.

[145]

However, it is well to be clear about the logical issues in testing theories concerning discriminating mechanisms.

If we assume that there are a number of systems working in parallel or in succession in visual recognition, then it is an inability to discriminate on the part of the animal which presents the strongest evidence for or against a hypothesis about the mechanism of one of the systems. If the animal cannot distinguish between two patterns, then it is clear that none of the systems concerned in visual recognition performs the discrimination. Therefore the system under consideration, which is one of the systems, does not perform the discrimination. If our hypothesis about this system leads us to predict that such a discrimination should be possible, we can then say that it is wrong. If, on the other hand, the animal can distinguish the two patterns and our hypothesis about one particular system would predict that such a discrimination is impossible for the system, it would be unreasonable to abandon our hypothesis. For another parallel system could be performing the discrimination. We need only say that it was bad luck from our point of view that other systems are present which mask the inadequacies of the system which we are considering. Thus we learn much more from failures than from successes.

The possibility that we are working with a discriminating system which has others to supplement it leads to other difficulties. One of these is the design of transfer experiments to test what shapes the animal treats as equivalent. The usual way to design such an experiment is to train the animal to learn to discriminate two shapes. After a certain criterion has been reached, one of the shapes is then substituted to see whether training breaks down or whether the substituted shape is treated partly or wholly as equivalent. The ability to transfer may be due to similarities registered in systems other than those in which we are interested. It is therefore a somewhat dubious criticism of a theory of shape discrimination that animals will transfer on the basis of the horizontal-vertical component if such a theory assumes that another system carries out this discrimination. Animals would, under other experimental conditions, transfer entirely on the brightness cue, an ability unaccounted for by a theory such as Dodwell's. But this would not constitute evidence against such a theory. In Dodwell's case, the pretraining with horizontal and vertical striations given to his animals would make transfer on a dimension irrelevant to a theory of pure shape recognition even more probable. Equally, a bias in favor of a theory such as his would be introduced. Dodwell takes the present writer to task for using evidence from Lashley's experiments in support of his own theory. He points out quite rightly that, under the circumstances of Lashley's experiments, the animals could have been using subsidiary cues, such as the shapes made with the boundary and part figures. However, the writer only used one finding of Lashley's, that being the rats' inability to distinguish squares from circles. While the utilization of subsidiary cues could have improved the rat's ability to distinguish, it is difficult to see how it could have impaired it, and that is why the present writer used the evidence. Dodwell's attempted explanation of the inability to discriminate in Lashley's situation is open to doubt. He suggests that the rat discriminates solid figures (as opposed to outlines) by the comparison of brightness in the various quadrants of the cards. He suggests that the brightness relationship in the various quadrants of a card containing a solid circle and solid square are the same. Therefore, as brightness is a "dominant" cue, the rat fails to discriminate. This line of reasoning would lead us to predict that rats could not discriminate a square from another rotated through 45°. However, Lashley found that rats could perform this discrimination.

Dodwell quotes the evidence of Gellermann asserting that chimpanzees did not have the ability to recognize rotated triangles as demanded by the writer's theory. However, Gellermann found that these animals and young children could recognize these figures when they were rotated. What Dodwell presumably means is that they did not make this discrimination without head rotation (as Hebb does). Dodwell's theory would predict that recognition could not be effected without the rotation of the receptors by an equal amount as the shapes (his third prediction). The writer's theory would predict that recognition would be possible without head rotation. (But as the organism would learn about the orientation of the shape as well, which would naturally be upset by the rotation of the shape, only partial overall similarity would result.) Do Gellermann's results favor Dodwell's theory or the writer's? Both the children and the chimpanzees did rotate their heads before making their choice, and their choice was correct. However, there are at least two interpretations of these findings. The first is that the subjects could not discriminate between the stimuli

[147]

until they had rotated their heads and that head rotation is a prerequisite of shape recognition in this situation. This interpretation would support Dodwell's theory, in which most rotations of shapes would destroy any "similarity" between them. The second interpretation is that the subjects only rotated their heads because they had already recognized the shape—and recognized it as rotated. The purpose of the head rotation is merely to turn a similarity into an identity. On this hypothesis, the rotation is the result of recognition, and not its precursor.

There are various points in Gellermann's account which support this second interpretation. If head rotation preceded the recognition of the rotated figure, then other substitutions of, or changes in, the figures besides rotations ought to have produced random head-turning movements. This was not the case. Gellermann carried out many different transfer tests (on some of which the subjects failed) and he states: "This head-turning behaviour was practically absent in tests other than those in which the rotation of figures took place" (p. 17). Further, it appears that the rotation of the head was highly purposive in such a way as to suggest that the figures were recognized as rotated. "In some cases it was quite comical to witness the positions taken by both the children and apes in viewing the rotated figures. They even went so far as to 'stand on their heads' on one or two occasions" (p. 17). A further observation, which suggests that recognition took place before head rotation, occurred when there was a test involving simultaneous rotation of the triangle and a substitution of negative figure. "All subjects continued to react positively to the triangle under these changed conditions. An interesting type of behaviour accompanied these correct responses. In every case the subjects hesitated on their trials under these new conditions, and, after looking from form to form, *they turned their heads about 60 degrees to one side or the other and viewed the triangle.* Then they made the correct response." This would seem to show fairly conclusively that recognition took place before rotation and not after. Otherwise we must explain why head-turning occurred only in relation to the correct figure and why it was practically absent in other transfer tests, even when discrimination broke down and both figures must have appeared strange. These observations give strong support to the second interpretation, especially as Gellermann himself missed their significance and subscribes to the first interpretation. They are,

[148]

therefore, the reports of an observer who was actually biased not to make them. It would, nevertheless, be desirable and easy to test these rival interpretations by a fresh experiment.

Gellermann used two children and two chimpanzees in his experiment. The present writer has carried out some observations on one child which suggest strongly that shapes can be recognized independent of rotation. The boy observed (J. A. D.) was 3 years and 1 month old when he began to take an interest in letters. He learned to write a capital *A* readily and would exclaim to point it out whenever he saw it. On one occasion when he was looking at a book he discovered a small *v*. He drew attention to it by saying: "Why is this *A* not crossed?" Similarly at the age of 3 years and 2 months he noticed a large *V* on a cardboard box and pointed it out as an *A*. No other confusions with an *A* were ever noted. The letter *A* had been pointed out to him only in the correct orientation.

At the age of 3 years and 2 months he began to imitate many capital letters and also discovered for himself how to write some of those he knew. This last category was of great interest. He discovered how to write *L* after having it pointed out to him. He wrote it as Γ and continues to do so (he is now 3 years, 3 months). This is unlikely to be due to a motor difficulty, as he could before this execute a capital *E*, which has both the correct and incorrect constituents. He can also execute a tolerable square.

He also at this age learned by a process of trial and error to write both a *T* and a *C* on their side. A *P* was spontaneously discovered and written entirely in the correct orientation. Though an *H* and *E* were usually written in the correct orientation, the *H* was occasionally turned on its side. The *E* has been written as � at a tilt of 25° from the horizontal (and also vertical). Tilts of such magnitude from their correct orientation were, and continue to be, very common. Care was taken not to show letters to the child in their incorrect orientation. In case it is thought that random errors have been picked out, it must be stressed that the errors mentioned were regular in their occurrence. Second, any errors in the shape (as apart from orientation), if they seemed to the child to alter the letter's appearance, caused him to cross the letter out by scribbling over it. Though it is not possible to define objectively the degree of distortion which gave rise to dissatisfaction, the fact is mentioned to show that the child would not accept just any shape as the equivalent of that which he intended to write.

It does not seem possible in the present state of the evidence to decide with any certainty which theory of shape recognition—Dodwell's, Sutherland's, or the writer's—is more likely to be correct. A preference for one or the other is based entirely on one's reading of ambiguous and sparse experimental evidence. It is to be hoped that the present controversy will stimulate more experimental research and sharpen the experimental designs used.

One of the most important points at issue is whether shapes can be recognized independent of rotation. If they can, then Dodwell's and Sutherland's systems lose a great deal of their plausibility. A system for shape recognition employing external axes against which the shapes are measured should emit drastically altered messages when shapes are rotated. The problem of finding an invariant among the family of messages generated by successive rotations of the same shape then arises. Without some means of estimating and compensating for the angle of tilt of the whole figure, it is difficult to envisage a solution. Even if such a means were adopted, it would mean that we should now have the task of virtually "rotating" the encoded shape. We might as well rotate the uncoded shape before, as Pitts and McCulloch have suggested. To do this rotation without encoding first would almost certainly be simpler.

On the writer's reading of the experimental evidence (especially Gellermann's, which has been discussed above) shapes can be recognized independent of rotation. On the other hand, there is much evidence that the inclination of lines can be discriminated by animals. If both these propositions are true, then it seems most economical to postulate two abstracting mechanisms, each with its own output. If we wish to obtain information about a shape independent of its tilt, we must in some way discard all information about its tilt. This is the very information we wish to inspect if we wish to know about tilt. If we have one encoding mechanism which passes out a message giving information both about shape and tilt, then we have a message which has still to be separated into the two components of shape and tilt, presumably by abstracting mechanisms further along. These abstracting mechanisms would have to perform virtually the same job as the two abstracting mechanisms suggested by the author, except that they would be inserted at a later stage. The difference would be that an earlier, transforming stage would have been inserted, translating the in-

[150]

formation about shape and tilt into another code. Such a scheme is clearly more elaborate. It has a stage which is not only superfluous but would also probably turn out to complicate the task of abstraction if the scheme was fully worked out.

Such is the writer's argument for postulating two mechanisms and at as early a stage as possible. Though the postulation of two distinct abstracting mechansims seems logically less parsimonious than the postulation of one, it is more economical mechanically. This is because the postulation of a single system turns out to be delusory as two systems are eventually needed and a single-system theory only postpones the real problem—that of abstracting the two types of information—to a later stage.

iv

A SYSTEM FOR SLANT DISCRIMINATION

A system for slant discrimination must pass out an identical message for lines which are parallel to each other, wherever they may lie on the receptor surface, and different outputs from lines at various degrees from the horizontal. The system suggested here converts the slant or tilt of a line on the retina into a frequency of channels stimulated per unit time by differentially delaying points, depending on their position on the receptor surface. Suppose that we have a bundle of channels in a cable (such as the optic nerve) each of which conducts a message at a certain speed. If the channels are of equal length but conduct at unequal speeds, or are of unequal lengths but conduct at equal speeds, then impulses traveling up these channels will take a different time to reach the end of each channel, even if they all start off at the same time and at the same place. If the lengths (or speeds) of these channels are arranged so that some channels have the same length or speed as adjacent channels, whereas others do not, then a fixed number of messages fed into channels of the same length and speed will arrive at the end of these channels simultaneously, but if the channels were different, then the messages will arrive at the end of the cable spread out in time. Let us suppose that the channels are systematically arranged so that those forming horizontal lines are of equal length. Then a group of messages placed on a horizontal row will arrive synchronously.

Further, if the channels increase in length from the bottom

[151]

horizontal row upward, so that each successive row contains cables longer than those of its vertical predecessor, then messages placed on a vertical row will arrive asynchronously. Let us further assume that the channels are so arranged that lines of equal length at whatever slant they are placed on the receptor surface stimulate the same number of channels. Thus a line placed at a given slant between the horizontal and the vertical will produce firing of a corresponding given frequency at the end of the cable.

If such messages are then conveyed with the same delay to a set of synaptic mechanisms of a type already described, the system will then discriminate tilt or slant.

For convenience we may regard the cable as cut slantwise so that the longer channels occur at the top of the visual field and the shorter at the bottom (see Fig. 26). The differential delay may not be effected by differential length, but by whatever factor

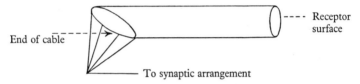

FIG. 26.—System for slant discrimination

it is effected, this factor can diagrammatically be represented by length.

In this simple system the tilt of a line is converted into a frequency of pulse arrival. This is obtained by relaying the components of the line down channels with a differential delay. The channels are so arranged that on one co-ordinate their delays are the same; on the other, so that their delays always increase. If the number of components of a line stays the same, whatever its slant (and this will depend on the arrangement and cross-section of the channels), then the number of components of the line which arrive per unit time depends only on its angle to the horizontal co-ordinate. Such a system would distinguish between horizontal and vertical lines and between these and lines at 45° to these. It would not distinguish between lines at 45° to the horizontal and their mirror image (if the mirror is placed at right angles to the horizontal).

Such an arrangement can discriminate between certain classes of outline, and appears to be chiefly responsible for shape recogni-

[152]

tion in the octopus. Here we can draw on the excellent experimental work by Dr. N. S. Sutherland. He finds that in general octopuses distinguish much more readily between figures which are mirror images of the upside-down variety, such as U and ∩, but find mirror images at right angles to the horizontal diffcult, for example, C and Ɔ. In the case of U and ∩, horizontal components would arrive, one at the beginning of a message and the other at the end. In the case of C and Ɔ, the horizontal components arrive at both the beginning and the end. In the case of V and Λ we should except a difficulty for both types of mirror image because here the rate of arrival of contour is the same for both figures in each pair. On the other hand, though V and a W as narrow as the V should appear alike, with the points upward or downward because the rate of arrival of contour components is the same, if the points are sideways the figures should be more readily discriminable, as the rate of arrival for a ⋛ is higher than for a <, though this will depend on the "acuity" for small differences in frequency. It is to be noted that the arrival of two contours at the same time would be treated (according to the scheme already set up) as being the same as the arrival of one contour at a frequency which is the sum of the two frequencies arriving. The information which is used is the total number of arrivals per unit time.

Two such systems at right angles to each other give discriminations which would not be prone to left-right confusions any more than to upward-downward confusions, but the indications are that this is not the case, at least in the octopus.

So far the connections to the synaptic frequency-sorting arrangements have not received much attention. It has been said simply that all the channels are collected together and conveyed with the same delay to the synaptic mechanism. A closer consideration will now be given to this problem. Evidently it would be wasteful to connect each channel in the cable to the synaptic arrangement. Only that number of outputs from the system has to be provided as there are cells capable of firing simultaneously at any one time. This number is given by the number of cells in one horizontal row. The system needs to report only the number of channels firing at any one time. Channels vertical to each other channot fire at the same time, and therefore they can share the same output connection. It is therefore highly probable that all the cells in a line at right angles to the horizontal are connected to the same output channel. This reduces the number of connections from the system substantially and suggests another interesting possibility.

Suppose that each channel or fiber was connected to the output channel (connecting the vertical rows) through a synapse (see Fig. 27) and that this output channel was itself interrupted by a synapse each time another channel or fiber from the receptor joined it, then the distance away from the frequency sorter on this channel would provide the differential delay for the vertical rows. If $a\,b\,c\,d\,e\,f$ arrive simultaneously, then f has one synaptic delay before it has its pulse sent to the frequency sorter. The pulse from the next channel, e, will have reached the output channel at the same time, but it has an extra synapse to cross after this before it too is finally sent to the frequency sorter with no more delay than the pulse from

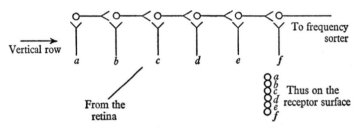

FIG. 27.—A possible synaptic delay mechanism

f. It is therefore tempting to suggest that the variations in delay between various channels are due to their mode of connection to an output channel in the way described.

If the number of output channels that has passed a message is counted after all the pulses have passed, the octopus will also be capable of making crude discriminations about the total extent of a figure on the horizontal axis and will not confuse ⌐ with ⊏ as it would otherwise do. However, such a mechanism on this axis is greatly inferior to the one dealing with vertical differences.

It is possible that in the case of the octopus there is no abstraction of outline when an inclosed figure is presented. If a figure is dealt with not as a set of contours but as a filled-in mass of points, then some of the predictions made from the theory will be different. For instance, there should be very little transfer from a solid figure to an outline figure. However, the system put forward above would still work but give some different results. It would be dealing with the number of points across the whole figure arriving per unit time, instead of the numbers of two points representing only the edges of the figure, arriving per unit time. It is conceivable that neither of these two limiting possibilities is actually used in the octopus. It is possible that the contour is merely accentuated (not being inhibited by excited points on one side) and that the points inside the figure are progressively more inhibited, so that some kind of intermediate possibility is actually dealt with. However, it is more likely that a greater rather than a lesser process of contour abstraction takes place on the system proposed, as this would greatly lessen the range of frequencies a frequency-sorting mechanism would have to cope with. Further, transfer from inclosed to uninclosed figures should be possible for the system. If it is possible, then the notion that the filled-in figures are dealt with can be rejected. If there is no transfer from an outline figure to a solid figure, then it can be said that the outline figure was somehow filled in, though it is difficult to see how. On the other hand, if there is transfer from an inverted outline triangle (▽), for instance, to a V shape on its side with top side horizontal (▷) then it is quite implausible to postulate a process of filling in.

If there is an abstraction of contour in the octopus, then it should have little difficulty in discriminating shape independent of the length or thickness of a line (provided always that the number of contours remains the same).

V

FIGURAL AFTEREFFECTS

In this section the applicability of some of the notions about the coding of the visual expanse will be demonstrated when we consider another set of phenomena in visual perception. First, however, the main theories concerning these phenomena will be discussed.

When a visual contour has been fixated for a minute or two, other contours placed in the vicinity are phenomenally shifted away from the locus of the first contour. This shift is not larger the nearer to each other the two contours are: the maximal aftereffect is secured when the two lines lie at a small distance from each other. This fact is known as the *distance paradox*. Though workers such as Gibson (1933) obtained such effects, it remained for Köhler and Wallach (1944) to investigate them thoroughly and to clarify

[155]

their genesis. Köhler and Wallach's empirical work on figural aftereffects, as these illusions are called, has largely been confirmed and extended; their theoretical interpretation has been hotly disputed. The neurophysiological assumptions peculiar to the theory have been amply criticized both experimentally and theoretically by Lashley *et al.* (1951).

Köhler and Wallach assume that the amount of flow of electrical current between two points in the visual projection area in the cortex is the correlate of seen distance between two points. It is further assumed that the flow of this current generated by a contour provides a hindrance to its own further flow, by an analogy with the raising of electrical resistance as a current progressively heats up a wire as it flows. Hence, as the "resistance" is raised at the locus and in the vicinity of a contour when it is fixated, the current passing between other contours placed in its vicinity should be affected. First, current should be deflected from the more "resistant" areas to those less so, so that contours both placed on one side, parallel to the locus of the fixated contour should appear closer together as the current emanating from the one closer to the area of heightened resistance should be forced to flow more in the direction of the decreased resistance. Hence, the amount of current flowing between these two contours will be larger and they will appear to be nearer together. Second, two contours placed on the two opposite sides parallel to the previously inspected contour should appear farther apart, as less current will be flowing between them. This is what is indeed observed. However, Hebb points out that, on this reasoning, contours placed at right angles parallel to each other on one side of the previously fixated contour should also seem to be farther apart from each other as the resistance between them has risen. But this is not the case, as Köhler and Wallach had themselves repeatedly observed. The opposite is the case. These contours are actually seen to be closer together. It therefore seems that the theory fails to account for one of the important facts.

The second main theory has been put forward by Osgood and Heyer (1953). These authors have made an attempt to construct a hypothesis consistent with what they take to be the facts of neurophysiology (that is, the speculations of Marshall and Talbot [1942]). This schema, it is claimed, can account for the facts observed equally as well as Köhler and Wallach's. Like many theories in psychology, such as Hull's (1952) and Hebb's (1949), it has implications which are never brought out by the author and which render the theory self-defeating.

Any theory of figural aftereffects has as its main task something which appears almost too simple—to explain why one line, after being exhibited for some time, begins to push all others away. Osgood and Heyer picture this in terms of a mechanism somewhat as follows.

In Osgood's words, the authors assume "that the apparent localization of a contour in subjective space coincides with the location of maximal excitation in area 17°" (Osgood, 1953, p. 236). "Drawing directly on the work of Marshall and Talbot (1942), we may assume that the representation of a contour in the projection cortex is a normal distribution of excitation symmetrical about its own axes transversely and extending as a 'ridge' through-

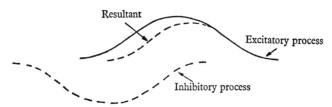

FIG. 28.—The inhibitory process interacting with the excitatory process from the first contour.

out the longitudinal extent of the contour." The shift in excitation representing another contour placed close to the locus of a previous one occurs because "under constant fixation of a figure, the cells in area 17 mediating the on-off activity will become differentially adapted as negatively accelerated functions of (a) the rate of their excitation and (b) the time through which they are excited" (Osgood, 1953, p. 238). Hence, "the locus of maximal rate of fire in the distribution representing a T-contour in subjective space can be shifted because of the differentially adapted region in which it falls" (p. 238). This would explain a shift. Unfortunately for the theory, it would also predict that such a shift could not be seen.

A contour, according to Osgood and Heyer, is "perceived" at the peak of a normal distribution of excitation. The shift in the second contour occurs because of an area of depressed excitability, left by the first, which will tend to show the second distribution of excitation, and its peak away from the first by a process of subtraction (see Fig. 28).

[157]

However, if we substitute the first contour for its inhibitory aftereffect, it will sum with the second to form a new peak (see Fig. 29).

It can be seen by inspection that if the two distributions are to subtract from each other successively, they will add up to a single peak if placed on the cortex simultaneously. Thus any interaction will occur only if the two contours are so near together as to be below the threshold of separation and any shift of a peak of excitation will in terms of visual distance be a mere fraction of this threshold. This unfortunate consequence is discussed at greater length by the writer (Deutsch, 1956a).

As neither of the above theories seems to be successful, the writer (Deutsch, 1956) put forward the following suggestion. He postulated that from each contour printed on the cortex emanates a wave

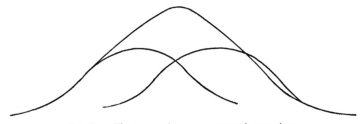

Fig. 29.—The two excitatory processes interacting

front which travels at a constant speed. When this wave front reaches another contour, a pulse is generated. If then a pulse is also generated when this wave front begins to travel, the time between the two pulses will be proportionate to the distance between the contours. This notion has already been used in the theory of shape recognition. Here it was assumed that an impulse is propagated from each part of a contour at right angles to its tangent.

When the contour is removed after a prolonged inspection, the tissue on which it has been represented will slow down any wave front passing over it. Around this refractory area there will be a fringe in the opposite state where a wave front will be conducted more speedily (see Fig. 30).

An alteration in the apparent distance between two lines is due to the altered time it takes for a wave front to travel between two points. The distance paradox is seen to be a consequence of whether the wave front has been exclusively speeded up or exclusively slowed down between two points by traveling only in a "faster" or only in a "slower" sector (see Fig. 31). As the wave front travels from A to B, the maximum time lost will be at B. Here will be the largest effect of "pushing away." Thereafter, as it travels to C, it will recover the time lost and its speed averaged for the whole distance from A to C will be nearer normal. Similarly, if the wave travels from B to C, the effect of B being pushed toward C would be much stronger than if contour B was placed nearer the locus of the previous contour. This would pull down the average speed nearer to normal and lessen the effect.

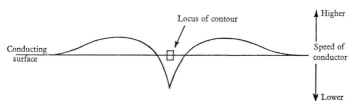

Fig. 30.—The effects of slowing down and speeding up around a contour

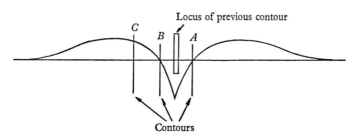

Fig. 31.—The effect of the origin of the wave front from the test figure

Further, the theory can explain the paradox which Hebb urged against Köhler and Wallach's theory. It is easy to see why two contours parallel to each other on one side of a previous contour at right angles to them should be seen as nearer together. The wave fronts emanating from them are passing over an area in which speeding up occurs, as shown in Figure 32.

The suppositions which have been made are no more unlikely than those made by Köhler and Wallach, or Osgood and Heyer, and they appear to account for the phenomena in a more satisfactory manner.

The difficulty which both previous theories have over the median

[159]

fissure seems to be more tractable on the present view. If an impulse has reached the edge and is conveyed from one hemisphere to the other sufficiently quickly and continues in the same direction, a functional unity is preserved. Furthermore, spatial distortions in the mapping of the retina or the cortex can be counteracted by differential rates of propagation over the cortex. Both these difficulties have been pointed out by Hebb.

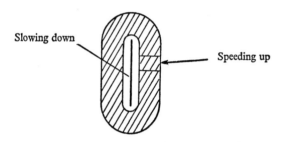

Slowing down

Speeding up

Fig. 32.—Areas of speeding up and slowing down around a contour

vi

THE AFTEREFFECTS OF SEEN MOVEMENT

When contours move over a certain part of the visual field and continue to do so in the same direction, then if they become stationary they appear to move in the opposite direction in that part of the visual field previously stimulated by the movement. Such an illusion is extremely powerful and striking. Wohlgemuth's monograph (1911) still remains the best account of it.

It has already been postulated that a contour generates wave fronts, traveling at a constant velocity away from it. To explain the perception of movement (at least in part) and its aftereffect, we must introduce the notion that these waves are generated by the contours at a steady repetition frequency. If two contours are stationary and they are the only contours in the visual field, then the waves emanating from one will reach the other at the normal rate (at the rate at which they were emitted). If they move in such a way that the distance that successive waves have to travel between them is unaltered, then they will again receive the waves at their normal frequency and the lines will appear statonary with respect to each other. If, on the other hand, they move in such a way that the distance between them is altered, the frequency of the received wave fronts will alter proportionately. There will be a frequency increase as they move nearer each other, and a decrease when they move away. This index of movement is dependent on the relative movement of the contours themselves and is not affected by eye movements which change the locus on the visual projection area but do not affect the relative position of the contours. It is the change in the relative positions which effects a change in the frequency received.

However, eye movements or the movements of the contours themselves (that is, movement relative to the receptor surface) will have another effect. This will be the rise or fall in the frequency of the passage of wave fronts traveling in a certain direction relative not to the contours but to a set of points on the receptor surface itself (or on the projection surface itself). As a movement in one direction occurs relative to the receptor surface, a contour, as it passes along, will generate a fresh wave front at successive points in its passage. It will be traveling in the same direction as one of the wave fronts it generates. If the contour had remained stationary, the wave fronts on either side of it would pass over a certain point on the projection surface at regular intervals, the intervals being those at which the wave front had been generated by the contour. But if the contour moves and generates another wave front after the usual interval, then the wave front which moves in the same direction as the contour had moved will pass over all the places in that direction much sooner after the previous wave front than if the contour had remained stationary. Similarly, the wave front passing in the other direction will pass much later after the previous wave front.

If contours pass over the same area of the visual field continuously in the same direction, then the elements passing the wave front in one direction will be stimulated at a rate higher than normal and those carrying it in the other, much less. It is to be noted that this alteration of frequency relative to a point on the projection surface can take place even if there is no alteration in the frequency from normal received by the contours. The frequency change in the case of the contours occurs because of their movement relative to each other; the frequency change over a part of the projection surface is due to a movement of the contour relative to it.

Let us suppose that a prolonged higher-than-normal stimulation of the processes propagating the wave fronts in a particular direction makes them more ready to fire at the normal rate. Then the transmission of the wave fronts in that particular direction will be at a higher velocity when the real movement in this direction ceases. If this higher velocity returns to normal after the cessation of this movement, then a change in the frequency of the arrival of wave fronts in that direction will also take place. If a wave travels more slowly than its predecessor, it will reach the same place later. Therefore a temporary decrease in frequency will take place of waves traveling in that direction in which motion previously took place. Any contour placed in this direction will therefore receive a lower frequency than the frequency of emission without a corresponding increase in frequency of the waves arriving from the other side. This occurs usually only when a contour is moving away from it. The direction of movement of the emitting contour relative to a stationary point will therefore appear to have reversed.

It is also a consequence of this theory that the time taken for a wave front to travel from one contour to another should be shorter when the contours are in movement but should increase after movement has stopped. This should have a corresponding effect on the apparent distance between the contours.

From this theory it would be predicted that the angular velocity (in terms of visual angle) of the spread of the postulated waves would be the same as the optimum angular velocity of movement which produces the aftereffect.

It must be stressed that the notion that distances and movements are partly measured in terms of traveling waves and their frequencies raises further problems which have not been dealt with. Only assumptions necessary for the explanation of the phenomena considered have so far been introduced.

XII

Concluding Remarks

i

REFLECTIVE

Here some of the sacred cows of psychology will be given a brisk hierological and veterinary examination. First, there are those with a slide rule; second, those with a scalpel. Such an examination is to some extent a defensive measure since these animals are redoubtable creatures.

The type of hypothesis or theory employed in the previous chapters is of a structural kind. The notions put forward do not represent statements about, or classifications of, behavior. The structure is described without an attempt to speculate about the neurological substrate, as a distinction is made between the structure and its embodiment.

No attempt is made to express the quantities in the system numerically. This may be regarded as a blemish. There is a prevalent feeling that any theory in psychology is not, properly speaking, scientific unless it is arithmetically formulated. The use of number within a theory is held somehow to make it like theories within the older established sciences. The introduction of theoretical systems which are qualitative and not quantitative may be thought to be a retrograde step. It is therefore worthwhile to examine some of the arguments which might be made for a numerical formulation of theory.

It may be said, for instance, that the introduction of exact numerical quantities into the system would render it more rigorous and precise. However, a distinction must be made between rigor and precision. A non-numerical system can be perfectly rigorous, though not quite as precise as a system employing number, if rigor is defined in terms of logical cogency. For instance, arguments in

[163]

Boolean algebra are logically rigorous insofar as the conclusions follow necessarily from the premises. It is possible to obtain such rigor in other systems without quantitative procedures. In this sense the theories put forward in the preceding chapters could be made completely rigorous, if they are not so already.

On the other hand, it is true that these theories are consistent with many more measurements of experimental results than theories which predict actual numerical data. In this sense the present theories are less precise. Similarly, it is very much more likely that the results predicted from these theories would turn up more often by chance. This means that they are much less sensitive to experimental disproof. Sensitivity to empirical evidence is held to be an important desideratum in a hypothesis. There are, however, qualifications to this requirement which ought to be made. There is no point in making our theories predict results within a smaller range of error than the accuracy of our measuring tools. If these are unreliable over a certain range, the exactness and precision of our theory is wasted. At worst, we may actually reject a hypothesis because it does not agree with a measurement whose accuracy is spurious. This could often be the case in psychology, where results may be biased in numberless small ways. It is not possible to control all the variables involved to the same extent as in physics. Therefore, results are always somewhat rough and represent only approximations. Each result then cannot be made to take too much weight and be treated as an accurate determination. There will always, of course, be disputes about this aspect of interpreting the evidence, depending on temperament and experience. The present author has played safe.

There is another side to this uncertainty about the precise result of an experiment. It makes it hazardous to use a result in calculating a quantitative aspect of a hypothetical system. Combined with other quantities derived from evidence with a similar range of uncertainty, deductions may be made predicting experimental outcomes which are wildly wrong. A theory could thus be discredited and rejected because it had been made prematurely too precise.

It is possible in such a case to go back and to alter the quantities built into the theory in order to save it. But if it is very likely that this will have to be the case, we may as well leave the quantities vague to begin with. There seems very little point in making guesses which are almost certainly wrong and clouding the issue just for the sake of investing a theory with an air of mock precision.

These arguments are not against quantification but against premature quantification. Can we say at all at what stage it is useful? We may begin by considering the whole universe of possible explanations of behavioral phenomena. These are not wholly independent of each other. They can be classified according to various principles. These classes have their further subdivisions. Experimental results narrow the field by excluding whole classes of alternative hypotheses and making others more plausible. Now, if the process of elimination of possibilities was the same as in a guessing game where the answer to each guess was "Yes" or "No," the process of guessing too far ahead would actually be wasteful. If the aim is to guess a word, it is uneconomical to guess our way through the dictionary. It is much more efficient to ask about the broader classes to which it could be assigned and gradually narrow these down. However, this comparison is to some extent misleading, as each experimental result gives us not only the answer "No," though it remains true that guessing too far ahead where successive subclassifications are concerned increases our chances of being wrong. In the case of a complex system where errors are multiplicative, even a modest attempt to be more precise can lead to astronomical odds against being precisely right. We can of course decide after experiment has been done whether this error is due to the data or whether it is the outline itself which is faulty. (But this decision may not always be easy.) However this may be, the details which have been inserted complicate the construction of the hypothesis and make prediction much more laborious. Whether this effort is merited is a matter of opinion. There seems, however, to be no advantage in inventing details before we are reasonably sure of the outline.

The insertion of quantities is an effort at classifying or defining a theory more precisely. In the case of the theories presented in the previous chapters there are experiments which can be done to test the hypotheses even if they are left unquantified. If the hypotheses are falsified, an attempt at their quantification will have merely wasted more time than had been wasted already. If they are verified we can then quantify. Precise quantities are further specifications of a qualitative system, and they do not need to be stated in order for us to decide that a range of systems qualitatively defined can be

[165]

excluded. For instance, if we have experimental evidence of shape recognition, we can exclude as being responsible the type of system operating in an adding machine, whatever its quantitative specifications.

The foregoing arguments against quantitative treatment are not directed against quantitative experimental work or theories of the generalization type which seek to summarize the data with a degree of precision not exceeding the reliability of the techniques employed in making the observations. The above considerations are adduced to show that a theory worked out in numerical detail is not methodologically or logically superior to its qualitative outline while this outline remains unconfirmed. Nothing is implied about the desirability of quantitative formulations in the future, but in the author's opinion they may turn out to be far less important than generally supposed. The types of system with properties reminiscent of those of living systems seems strangely independent of precise numerical properties. But the author does not wish to be misunderstood. He is convinced that quantitative formulations of theories are desirable in the long run, but only after we have made sure that the theories we are quantifying are qualitatively correct. A theory may still be wrong, however precisely it is expressed. Behaviorism concentrated on precision prematurely, to the exclusion of qualities which make precision a virtue only after they have already been exercised.

The author also believes that quantitative measurement, insofar as it gives a more accurate description of the behavior of the animal, is desirable. It is the behavior of the animal that psychological theories attempt to explain, and therefore it must be accurately known. His belief does not extend to psychological measuring scales which purport to measure such things as drive or learning. It seems that the motives behind these attempts need examining. It is often alleged that we must measure before we can explain and the example of the physical sciences is invoked. In these, progress was made when such things as temperature or time began to be accurately measured. This is true but misleading. The measures which were introduced allowed the scientist to describe more accurately the behavior of the systems which he was investigating. This is not the case with the psychological measuring scale. There is no difficulty about producing an accurate description of the physical behavior of an organism (and it is this we are attempting to explain) without a psychological scale. Indeed it would be impossible to apply a psychological scale without such a description of the physical behavior of the organism. This is all we need to describe the animal's behavior; all else is superfluous and misleading.

Second, we shall examine experimental neurology with relevance to its service in constructing explanations in terms of structure. It is notorious that all facts are not equally useful in solving a problem. Given that the animal is a type of mechanism, there are various ways in which we can find out about its internal structure. The first is to inspect the mechanism and work out the arrangement from the anatomical disposition. There are practical difficulties in the way here. But, disregarding these, we should also have to know the behavior of the individual units composing the structure. The anatomical disposition of these units without a knowledge of their properties cannot shed much light on the overall system. Another direct approach is to observe or manipulate changes within the internal structure to see how they correspond with changes in behavior. Such a neurophysiological approach is the most direct one logically. How far it is also practicable remains to be seen.

A second main way, less direct but scientifically more practicable and highly developed, lies through experimental psychology. This consists in discovering the properties of the organism by subjecting it to various tests. From the results of these tests we attempt to infer the system operating inside. Our hypothesis about the system employed can further be tested by verifying the predictions stemming from the hypotheses.

The two methods which promise to be of help are the inferential one, where one infers from the properties to the structure, and, second, the method of direct inspection, where we attempt to ascertain the structure or system by observing it directly, without arguing from behavior. The situation is similar to that to be found in man-made mechanisms. Both the methods outlined above are useful when we attempt to find out how a machine works. The distinction between these two complementary methods corresponds roughly to the type of investigations done by physiologists, on one side, and psychologists, on the other. However, this is not entirely so. It might appear that the distinction lies in working with the intact animal and adopting some means of surgery, or the like. However, it is not the difference between opening the "black box," to prod about inside, and watching what the black box does under various circumstances. The distinction is not based upon a physical procedure but on the logical status of the evidence obtained by the physical procedure, whatever this may be. Are we observing the structure or system directly, or are we merely observing the consequences of having such-and-such a structure? This is the question to be asked.

Now this opening of the box has become confused with direct observation of the system. Opening the box may enable us to observe the works directly and this, of course, is the royal road to explaining the behavior of the box. But opening the box does not of itself procure a superior brand of information. We can open the box and yet with certain techniques obtain information which is of the indirect kind and which may actually be more difficult to interpret than observations about the intact box—and so less valuable. This is the sort of information which is gained when we damage the mechanism inside the box to see what difference this makes to its behavior. Here we do not obtain direct evidence about the mechanism. We can only infer what the mechanism is from the subsequent behavior of the mutilated machine. This ablation technique is therefore not on a par with direct observation of the system. It is like the conventional observational evidence ordinarily collected by the experimental psychologist insofar as we can only infer from it. The data obtained stand in a similar logical relationship to the underlying structure, as do the data obtained with an intact organism. They are therefore not more direct. The superiority of ablation studies to conventional experiments with intact organisms may thus be doubted. All we seem to do by performing an ablation is to add an extra parameter to our results. Instead of writing, "An organism behaves x-wise in situation y," we say, "An organism behaves x-wise in situation y with lesion z." In this way we can correlate the geography of lesions with a symptomatology of behavior. In doing this, we are merely noting the consequences of not having such-and-such a structure. We are not observing the structure itself.

So far it has been shown that the technique of experimenting with brain lesions or ablations is not the direct one which it on the surface appears to be, and much more like the conventional technique of work with intact animals in the type of evidence it produces. However, it might be that the type of information we obtain through ablation studies is particularly valuable in helping us to form inferences about the system whose behavior we are observing.

[168]

If we can argue by analogy from practical experience with circuitry, the very opposite seems to be the case. The writer became interested in the status of ablation studies because he was struck with the inutility of analogous procedures in providing worthwhile information if we try to apply them to machines. These difficulties are shared by other psychologists with an experience of electronics with whom he has discussed the matter. The difficulty of making use of data from ablation-type procedures in making inferences about a system is due, it seems, to an inherent shortcoming of the data themselves. This can be brought out by the following argument. In general the fewer interpretations a fact is consistent with, the better evidential value it has. The facts we usually pick on as significant as opposed to facts which are meaningless are those which are consistent with a narrower range of possibilities. Now it seems to be the case, when we interfere with the structure by extracting a part whose absence may affect the rest of the system in any number of ways, that any piece of behavior which the truncated system now manifests is open to a considerably greater number of interpretations than the intact system in the same situation. Our interpretation of the behavior of the altered system can begin only when we have decided in what way the original system has been altered, not behaviorally, but in its working. We do not have to interpose this stage of uncertainty when interpreting the behavior of the intact system. It would, therefore, seem that evidence derived from ablation studies is not only as indirect an indication of a system but a great deal more so. So far from being evidence which is on a par with neurophysiology, it appears to be a great deal worse than the usual run of experimental results with intact animals, if we wish to pursue an explanation in terms of system or structure.

The study of the various bizarre symptoms which emerge after brain damage has its undoubted fascination. The evidential value of these disorders appears somewhat dubious for the theorist and experimentalist alike. Their relative valuelessness as information is not due to the stage at which the subject finds itself. They are always bound, by the logic of the thing, to be of a lower grade as evidence than behavior displayed by the intact animal. If one is to have some kind of scientific strategy, then the conventional techniques of work with animals with brain intact would seem to be far more valuable and promising. The same arguments can be applied to work with drugs, the so-called pharmacological lesions. However,

[169]

we must not conclude that the lesion technique is completely useless. It is possible to discover certain types of facts with its aid. For instance, we can sometimes conclude that two separate systems are responsible for carrying out a complex function for which a unitary system may have been thought responsible. Such evidence is on occasion very valuable. Further, ablation may tell us where to proceed with more sophisticated methods of observation. It would be foolish to deny that ablation has its place among the other techniques in helping us to form inferences about the system we are endeavoring to understand. The question we have been examining is only, "What is this place?" and "How large is it?"

ii

RETROSPECTIVE

There are some omissions in the preceding chapters which might be questioned. These concern the content rather than the form of the theories. No explanation has been given of aversive behavior, and no mention has been made of secondary drives. These omissions are to some extent linked together. Avoidance behavior is omitted because a different type of system appears to be responsible. The learning occurring as a part of avoidance behavior seems to be much more persistent and has different characteristics as far as extinction goes. An animal learns to fear the white box in which it has been shocked, and this fear persists for far longer than would be the case with an attraction, if the animal had been rewarded there. This phenomenon has been called a learned, or secondary, drive. The animal, so the theory runs, has acquired a drive when it now avoids the white box. (It would seem to be more natural to speak of the animal learning to fear a new object, namely, a white box. The learning seems more related to the object of the fear than to the fear, and it would seem that the "theory" is often just an odd, perhaps improper, way of talking.) This notion that drives can be learned owes it origin not so much to any observations on motivation but to the motivation of the proponents themselves. Starting from a doctrine which regards unlearned rewards as the reduction in some type of physiological deficit or avoidance of tissue damage, they nevertheless felt impelled to apply their laws to human behavior. It is notorious, however, that man indulges in such biologically unrewarding activities as philately. Further, the process of

[170]

social learning seems to have no frequent primary reinforcement. As it is for some obscure reason thought to be a stigma to have a theory which applies to rats alone, the theory was stretched to cover these somewhat remote human cases. It was proposed that all these rewards were those of drives which had been acquired, though no really analogous cases were found in the rat. There was the verbal case (to be found in the white box discussed above), but even this applied, strictly speaking, only to avoidance behavior. It is worth quoting Hull's first corollary, entitled "Secondary Motivation":

> When neutral stimuli are repeatedly and consistently associated with the evocation of a primary or secondary drive and this drive stimulus undergoes an abrupt diminution the hitherto neutral stimuli acquire the capacity to bring about the drive stimuli (S_D) which thereby become the condition (C_D) of a secondary drive or motivation.

It should be stressed that the only convincing evidence adduced in support of this corollary comes from the field of avoidance behavior. The work on this subject relevant to appetitive behavior is at present consistent with many other explanations and needs extending and repeating.

On the present view the supposition that drives may be acquired is unnecessary. The factor leading to reinforcement on this view is the arrival of a stimulus and not the termination of a deficit. Accordingly, we may suppose that social training is achieved, not through the operation of secondary drives, but by the primary reward value of such stimuli as smiles. The various signs of approval may be just as rewarding as food for a human child.

Such assertions, of course, do not follow as predictions from the system put forward; they flow more as suggestions, as possibilities made plausible by the frame of reference adopted.

For the reader who has remained unmoved by the above plea for the author's general approach, it may be well to review the various points of theoretical detail dealt with in the preceding pages which stand or fall individually in their own right. First, there is the reversal of the role of stimulation or afferent impulse in appetitive activity. It is suggested that stimulation in the case of "needs" does not set off activity but switches it off. This quite apart from the detailed working-out presented here may be a worthwhile notion. Stimulation in the case of goal-seeking activities is also not thought of as the trigger of a response but as an indicator of error

[171]

and as a signal which impedes the flow of excitation. It may be useful to keep these possibilities in mind, especially as it seems almost impossible to think of a stimulus as something which does not eventuate in a response.

The second group of ideas is concerned with the registration and selection of information during learning and performance, respectively. It is suggested that during learning receptors are arranged in a series according to the order in which they were stimulated. That is, the receptors are not joined to effectors or yet to other receptors, but are assigned a certain rank determined by the order in which they fired. The changing environment is subjected to a complex classification. The order of arrival of the various classes is noted. This is done by connecting the special structures to which the classifying systems are attached in the order in which they fired. These classes of stimulation, when the animal is motivated subsequently, serve as goals. Excitation flows from the part of the structure to which the final goal is fastened. This excitation is transmitted to other parts of the structure to which the receptors which were fired off previous to the attainment of this goal are fixed. These are in this way made goals in their turn. Through the approximation to these intermediate goals the animal attains its final aim.

Having stored the order in which receptors were set off, the animal can utilize the sequence to gain its objectives. This notion is developed if we assume that the excitation to be found in one sequence travels to another through a structure shared in common. This greatly extends the system's versatility in applying learned habits. This hypothesis, even if it proves wrong on points of detail, may be worth elaborating in other contexts. The role of stimulation as reward has already been alluded to.

So far most of the suggestions relate to learning and performance. However, there are some which concern the classification of the environment. It would seem true to say that most of these classifications are of relations. Though it appears easy enough to classify a set of particulars, the perception of relations has always been a baffling problem. This has been the case especially with shape recognition. It has been suggested by others that recognition here is effected by a conversion of a spatial extent into a temporal sequence. But there has been the assumption, clung to on the analogy of television, that the scan was along fixed co-ordinates independent of the figure to be coded or transformed. The notion peculiar to the suggestion here is that the outline of the figure itself acts as the origin of the transformation process. This general suggestion would seem to have important advantages and to be helpful in the explanation of other visual phenomena such as the aftereffects of seen movement.

The author hopes that the suggestions made in this book will prove of value especially to the neurophysiologist. A psychological theory of the structural kind based on behavior, distils for the physiologist all the welter and wealth of psychological experiment and draws attention to the type of functional interrelationships he should expect to find among his elements because of the interrelationships found in another province by the experimental psychologist. In this way the two disciplines can become truly complementary. The psychologist can, by inference from the behavior of the system, suggest hypotheses which the physiologist, helped by knowing what types of phenomena to look for, can then confirm by direct observation. On the other hand, the physiologist's observations, the significance of which may be obscure to him, can suggest to the psychologists the type of hypotheses which could account for certain behavior, and this he can go on to test by making behavioral predictions. In this way the psychologist and the physiologist can work together, the psychologist relieved of the necessity of physiological speculation and the neurophysiologist presented with actual hypotheses which he can test.

An attempt has been made to give a coherent explanation of some of the phenomena which the experimental psychologists have studied. The value of this attempt will be disputed. There are many psychologists who consider that their task is simply the accumulation of experimental data on problems which they feel are "interesting." This emphasis on experiment is no doubt a reaction from the armchair theorizing which was once fashionable. It was healthy to settle theoretical issues with an appeal to empirical evidence. It seems that the reaction has swung too far and that experimental data are now accumulated for their own sake, in some hope that when we have collected enough, their explanation will somehow become clear. But facts do not speak for themselves; they must be interpreted.

References

ANAND, B. K., and BROBECK, J. R. 1951. "Hypothalamic Control of Food Intake," *Yale J. Biol. Med.*, **24**, 123–40.

ANDERSSON, B. 1953. "The Effect of Injections of Hypertonic NaCL Solutions into Different Parts of the Hypothalamus of Goats," *Acta Physiol. Scand.*, **28**, 188–201.

ANDERSSON, B., and McCANN, S. M. 1955. "A Further Study of Polydipsia Evoked by Hypothalamic Stimulation in the Goat," *Acta Physiol. Scand.*, **33**, 333–46.

———. 1955. "Drinking, Antidiuresis and Milk Ejection from Electrical Stimulation from the Hypothalamus of Goats," *ibid.*, **35**, 191–201.

———. 1956. "The Effect of Hypothalamic Lesions on the Water Intake of the Dog," *ibid.*, pp. 312–20.

BARKER, J. P., ADOLPH, E. F., and KELLER, A. D. 1953. "Thirst Tests in Dogs and Modification of Thirst with Experimental Lesions of the Neurohypophysis," *Amer. J. Physiol.*, **173**, 233–45.

BASH, K. W. 1939. "An Investigation into a Possible Organic Basis for the Hunger Drive," *J. Comp. Psychol.*, **28**, 109–34.

BEACH, F. A. 1948. *Hormones and Behavior: A Survey of Interrelationships between Endocrine Secretions and Patterns of Overt Response.* New York: Paul B. Hoeber.

BELLOWS, R. T. 1939. "Time Factors in Water Drinking in Dogs," *Amer. J. Physiol.*, **125**, 87–97.

BERKUN, M. M., KESSEN, MARION L., and MILLER, N. E. 1952. "Hunger-reducing Effects of Food by Stomach Fistula versus Food by Mouth Measured by a Consummatory Response," *J. Comp. Physiol. Psychol.*, **45**, 550–55.

BERLYNE, D. E. 1950. "Novelty and Curiosity as Determinants of Exploratory Behaviour," *Brit. J. Psychol.*, **41**, 68–80.

———. 1955. "The Arousal and Satiation of Perceptual Curiosity in the Rat," *J. Comp. Physiol. Psychol.*, **48**, 238–46.

BERLYNE, D. E., and SLATER, J. 1957. "Perceptual Curiosity, Exploratory Behavior and Maze Learning," *J. Comp. Physiol. Psychol.*, **50**, 228–31.

[175]

BIRCH, H. G. 1945. "The Relation of Previous Experience to Insightful Problem Solving," *J. Comp. Psychol.*, **38**, 367–83.

BOLLES, R., and PETRINOVICH, L. 1954. "A Technique for Obtaining Rapid Drive Discrimination in the Rat," *J. Comp. Physiol. Psychol.*, **47**, 378–80.

BURNS, B. D. 1950. "Some Properties of the Cat's Isolated Cerebral Cortex," *J. Physiol.*, **111**, 50–68.

——. 1951. "Some Properties of Isolated Cerebral Cortex in the Unanaesthetised Cat," *ibid.*, **112**, 156–75.

BURNS, B. D., and GRAFSTEIN, B. 1952. "The Function and Structure of Some Neurones in the Cat's Cerebral Cortex," *J. Physiol.*, **118**, 412–33.

CALDWELL, W. E., and JONES, H. B. 1954. "Some Positive Results on a Modified Tolman and Honzik Insight Maze," *J. Comp. Physiol. Psychol.*, **47**, 416–18.

CARPER, J. W., and POLLIARD, F. 1953. "A Comparison of the Intake of Glucose and Saccharine Solutions under Conditions of Caloric Need," *Amer. J. Psychol.*, **66**, 478–82.

CHAMBERS, R. M. 1956a. "Effects of Intravenous Glucose Injections on Learning, General Activity, and Hunger Drive," *J. Comp. Physiol. Psychol.*, **49**, 558–64.

——. 1956b. "Some Physiological Bases for Reinforcing Properties of Reward Injections," *ibid.*, pp. 565–68.

COPPOCK, H. W., and CHAMBERS, R. M. 1954. "Reinforcement of Position Preference by Automatic Intravenous Injections of Glucose," *J. Comp. Physiol. Psychol.*, **47**, 355.

DEESE, J. 1951. "The Extinction of a Discrimination without Performance of a Choice Response," *J. Comp. Physiol. Psychol.*, **44**, 362–66.

DEMBER, W. N. 1956. "Response by the Rat to Environmental Change," *J. Comp. Physiol. Psychol.*, **49**, 93–95.

DENNIS, W. 1939. "Spontaneous Alternation in Rats as an Indication of the Persistence of Stimulus Effects," *J. Comp. Psychol.*, **28**, 305–12.

DE SNOO, K. 1937. "Das trinkende Kind im Uterus," *Monatschrift f. Geburtsch u. Gynäk*, **105**, 88.

DEUTSCH, J. A. 1953. "A New Type of Behaviour Theory," *Brit. J. Psychol.*, **44**, 304–17.

——. 1955. "A Theory of Shape Recognition," *ibid.*, **46**, 30–37.

——. 1956. "A Theory of Insight, Reasoning and Latent Learning," *ibid.*, **47**, 115–25.

——. 1956a. "The Statistical Theory of Figural After-effects and Acuity," *ibid.*, pp. 208–15.

——. 1957. "Nest Building Behaviour of Domestic Rabbits under Semi-natural Conditions," *Brit. J. Animal. Behav.*, **5**, 53–54.

[176]

———. 1958. "Double Drive Learning without Previous Selective Reinforcement," *Quart. J. Exper. Psychol.*, **10**, 207–10.

———. 1959. "The Hull-Leeper Drive Discrimination Situation—a Control Experiment," *Quart. J. Exper. Psychol.*, **11**, 155–63.

DEUTSCH, J. A., and ANTHONY, W. 1958. "Blocking the Incorrect Alley in a Two-Drive Learning Situation," *Quart. J. Exp. Psychol.*, **10**, 22–28.

DEUTSCH, J. A., and CLARKSON, J. K. 1959*a*. "Nature of the Vibrato and the Control Loop in Singing," *Nature*, **183**, 167–68.

———. 1959*b*. "Reasoning in the Hooded Rat," *Quart. J. Exper. Psychol.*, **11**, 150–54.

———. 1959*c*. "A Test of the Neo-behavioristic Theory of Extinction," *Quart. J. Exper. Psychol.*, **11**, 155–63.

DEUTSCH, J. A., and JONES, A. D. 1959. "The Water-Salt Receptor and Preference in the Rat," *Nature*, **183**, 1472.

DODWELL, P. C. 1957. "Shape Recognition in Rats," *Brit. J. Psychol.*, **48**, 221–29.

ELAM, C. B., TYLER, D. W., and BITTERMAN, M. E. 1954. "A Further Study of Secondary Reinforcement and the Discrimination Hypothesis," *J. Comp. Physiol. Psychol.*, **47**, 381–84.

EPSTEIN, A. N., and STELLAR, E. 1955. "The Control of Salt Preference in the Adrenalectomised Rat," *J. Comp. Physiol. Psychol.*, **48**, 167–72.

EVANS, S. 1936. "Flexibility of Established Habit," *J. Gen. Psychol.*, **14**, 177–200.

FULLER, J. L., and JACOBY, S. A., JR. 1955. "Central and Sensory Control of Food Intake in Genetically Obese Mice," *Amer. J. Physiol.*, **183**, 279–83.

GELLERMANN, L. W. 1933. "Form Discrimination in Chimpanzees and Two-Year-Old Children. I. Form (Triangularity) *Per Se*," *J. Genet. Psychol.*, **42**, 3–27.

GIBSON, J. J. 1933. "Adaptation, After-effect and Contrast in the Perception of Curved Lines," *J. Exper. Psychol.*, **16**, 1–31.

GLANZER, M. 1953. "Stimulation Satiation: An Explanation of Spontaneous Alternation and Related Phenomena," *Psychol. Rev.*, **60**, 257–68.

GLEITMAN, H. 1955. "Place Learning without Prior Performance," *J. Comp. Physiol. Psychol.*, **48**, 77–79.

GOTTSCHALDT, K. 1926. "Ueber den Einfluss der Erfahrung auf die Wahrnehmung von Figuren," *Psychol. Forsch.*, **8**, 261–317.

GRICE, G. R. 1948. "An Experimental Test of the Expectation Theory of Learning," *J. Comp. Physiol. Psychol.*, **41**, 137–43.

GUTTMAN, N. 1954. "Equal Reinforcement Values for Sucrose and Glucose Solutions Compared with Equal Sweetness Values," *J. Comp. Physiol. Psychol.*, **47**, 358–61.

[177]

HAMMER, E. R. 1949. "Temporal Factors in Figural After-effects," *Amer. J. Psychol.*, **62**, 337–54.

HEATHERS, G. L. 1940. "The Avoidance of Repetition of a Maze Reaction in the Rat as a Function of the Time Interval between Trials," *J. Psychol.*, **10**, 359–80.

HEBB, D. O. 1949. *The Organization of Behavior: A Neuropsychological Theory.* New York: John Wiley & Sons.

HICK, W. E. 1952. "On the Rate of Gain of Information," *Quart. J. Exper. Psychol.*, **4**, 11–26.

HINDE, R. A., THORPE, W. H., and VINCE, M. A. 1956. "The Following Response of Young Coots and Moorhens," *Behaviour*, **9**, 214–42.

HULL, C. L. 1933. "Differential Habituation to Internal Stimuli in the Albino Rat," *J. Comp. Psychol.*, **16**, 255–73.

———. 1935. "The Mechanism of the Assembly of Behavior Segments in Novel Combinations Suitable for Problem Solutions," *Psychol. Rev.*, **42**, 219–45.

———. 1943. "The Problem of Intervening Variables in Molar Behavior Theory," *ibid.*, **50**, 273–91.

———. 1951. *Essentials of Behavior.* New Haven, Conn.: Yale University Press.

———. 1952. *A Behavior System.* New Haven, Conn.: Yale University Press.

HULL, C. L., LIVINGSTON, F. R., ROUSE, R. O., and BARKER, A. N. 1951. "True, Sham, and Esophageal Feeding as Reinforcements," *J. Comp. Physiol. Psychol.*, **44**, 236–45.

HUTT, P. J. 1954. "Rate of Bar Pressing as a Function of Quality and Quantity of Food Reward," *J. Comp. Physiol. Psychol.*, **47**, 235–39.

KAGAN, J. 1955. "Differential Reward Value of Incomplete and Complete Sexual Behavior," *J. Comp. Physiol. Psychol.*, **48**, 59–64.

KENDLER, H. H. 1946. "The Influence of Simultaneous Hunger and Thirst Drives upon the Learning of Two Opposed Spatial Responses of the White Rat," *J. Exper. Psychol.*, **36**, 212–20.

———. 1947. "A Comparison of Learning under Motivated and Satiated Conditions in the White Rat," *ibid.*, **37**, 545–49.

———. 1947. "An Investigation of Latent Learning in a T-Maze," *J. Comp. Physiol. Psychol.*, **40**, 265–70.

KENDLER, H. H., and MENCHER, H. C. 1948. "The Ability of Rats To Learn the Location of Food when Motivated by Thirst—an Experimental Reply to Leeper," *J. Exper. Psychol.*, **38**, 82–88.

KIVY, P. N., EARL, R. W., and WALKER, E. L. 1956. "Stimulus Context and Satiation," *J. Comp. Physiol. Psychol.*, **49**, 90–92.

KLÜVER, H. 1927. "Visual Disturbances after Cerebral Lesions," *Psychol. Bull.*, **24**, 316–58.

Koch, S. 1954. In *Modern Learning Theory*, ed. W. K. Estes. New York: Appleton-Century-Crofts.

Köhler, W., and Wallach, H. 1944. "Figural After-effects," *Proc. Amer. Phil. Soc.*, **88**, 269–357.

Kohn, M. 1951. "Satiation of Hunger from Food Injected Directly into the Stomach versus Food Ingested by Mouth," *J. Comp. Physiol. Psychol.*, **44**, 412–22.

Lashley, K. S. 1938. "The Mechanism of Vision. XV. Preliminary Studies of the Rat's Capacity for Detail Vision," *J. Gen. Psychol.*, **18**, 123–93.

Lashley, K. S., Chow, K. L., and Semmes, Josephine. 1951. "An Examination of the Electrical Field Theory of Cerebral Integration," *Psychol. Rev.*, **58**, 123–351.

Leeper, R. 1935. "The Role of Motivation in Learning: A Study of the Phenomenon of Differential Motivational Control of the Utilization of Habits," *J. Genet. Psychol.*, **46**, 3–40.

Lehrman, D. S. 1953. "A Critique of Konrad Lorenz's Theory of Instinctive Behavior," *Quart. Rev. Biol.*, **28**, 337–63.

Lilly, J. C., and Cherry, R. B. 1954. "Surface Movements of Click Responses from Acoustic Cerebral Cortex of Cat: Leading and Trailing Edges of a Response Figure," *J. Neurophysiol.*, **17**, 521–32.

Lorenz, K. Z. 1950. "The Comparative Method in Studying Innate Behaviour Patterns," *Physiological Mechanisms in Animal Behaviour* ("Symp. Soc. Exper. Biol.," No. IV), pp. 221–68. Cambridge: Cambridge University Press.

McAllister, W. R. 1952. "The Spatial Relation of Irrelevant and Relevant Goal Objects as a Factor in Simple Selective Learning," *J. Comp. Physiol. Psychol.*, **45**, 531–37.

MacCorquodale, K., and Meehl, P. E. 1948. "On a Distinction between Hypothetical Constructs and Intervening Variables," *Psychol. Rev.*, **55**, 95–107.

McNamara, H. J., Long, J. B., and Wike, E. L. 1956. "Learning without Response under Two Conditions of External Cues," *J. Comp. Physiol. Psychol.*, **49**, 477–80.

Maier, N. R. F. 1929. "Reasoning in White Rats," *Comp. Psychol. Monogr.*, Vol. **6**, No. 29.

Marshall, W. H., and Talbot, S. A. 1942. "Recent Evidence for Neural Mechanisms in Vision Leading to a General Theory of Sensory Acuity," in *Visual Mechanisms*, ed. H. Klüver. Lancaster, Pa.: Jaques Cattell Press.

Meehl, P. E., and MacCorquordale, K. 1948. "A Further Study of Latent Learning in the T-Maze," *J. Comp. Physiol. Psychol.*, **41**, 372–96.

Miller, N. E. 1957 "Experiments on Motivation Studies Combining

Psychological, Physiological and Pharmacological Techniques," *Science*, **126**, 1271–78.

MILLER, N. E., BAILEY, C. J., and STEVENSON, J. A. F. 1950. "Decreased 'Hunger' but Increased Food Intake Resulting from Hypothalamic Lesions," *Science*, **112**, 256–59.

MILLER, N. E., and KESSEN, MARION L. 1952. "Reward Effects of Food via Stomach Fistula Compared with Those of Food via Mouth," *J. Comp. Physiol. Psychol.*, **45**, 555–64.

———. 1954. "Is Distention of the Stomach by a Balloon Rewarding or Punishing?" *Amer. Psychologist*, **9**, 430–31.

MILLER, N. E., SAMPLINER, R. I., and WOODROW, P. 1957. "Thirst-reducing Effects of Water by Stomach Fistula vs. Water by Mouth Measured by Both a Consummatory and an Instrumental Response," *J. Comp. Physiol. Psychol.*, **50**, 1–6.

MOLTZ, H. 1957. "Latent Extinction and the Fractional Anticipatory Response Mechanism," *Psych. Rev.*, **64**, 229–41.

MONTGOMERY, K. C. 1951. "The Relation between Exploratory Behavior and Spontaneous Alteration in the White Rat," *J. Comp. Physiol. Psychol.*, **44**, 582–89.

———. 1952. "A Test of Two Explanations of Spontaneous Alternation," *ibid.*, **45**, 287–93.

———. 1952. "Exploratory Behavior and Its Relation to Spontaneous Alternation in a Series of Maze Exposures," *ibid.*, 50–57.

———. 1953. "Exploratory Behavior as a Function of 'Similarity' of Stimulus Situations," *ibid.*, **46**, 129–33.

———. 1954. "The Role of Exploratory Drive in Learning," *ibid.*, **47**, 60–64.

MONTGOMERY, M. F. 1931. "The Role of Salivary Glands in the Thirst Mechanism," *Amer. J. Physiol.*, **96**, 221–27.

MUNN, N. L. 1950. *Handbook of Psychological Research on the Rat.* Boston: Houghton Mifflin Co.

NORTON, FAY, TYLER, M., and KENSHALO, D. R. 1954. "Incidental Learning under Conditions of Unrewarded Irrelevant Motivation," *J. Comp. Physiol. Psychol.*, **47**, 375–77.

OLDS, J. 1958. "Self Stimulation of the Brain," *Science*, **127**, 315–24.

OSGOOD, C. E. 1953. *Method and Theory in Experimental Psychology.* New York: Oxford University Press.

OSGOOD, C. E., and HEYER, A. W. 1951. "A New Interpretation of Figural After-effects," *Psychol. Rev.*, **59**, 98–118.

SEWARD, J. P., and LEVY, N. 1949. "Sign Learning as a Factor in Extinction," *J. Exper. Psychol.*, **39**, 660–68.

SHANNON, CLAUDE E. 1938. "A Symbolic Analysis of Relay and Switching Circuits," *Transactions Amer. Inst. Electrical Engineers*, **57**, 1–11.

SHEFFIELD, F. D., and ROBY, T. B. 1950. "Reward Value of Non-nutritive Sweet Taste," *J. Comp. Physiol. Psychol.*, **43**, 471–81.

SHEFFIELD, F. D., ROBY, T. B., and CAMPBELL, B. A. 1954. "Drive Reduction versus Consummatory Behavior as Determinants of Reinforcement," *J. Comp. Physiol. Psychol.*, **47**, 349–54.

SHEFFIELD, F. D., WULFF, J. J., and BACKER, R. 1951. "Reward Value of Copulation without Sex Drive Reduction," *J. Comp. Physiol. Psychol.*, **44**, 3–8.

SIDMAN, M., BRADY, J. V., BOREN, J. J., CONRAD, D. G., and SCHULMAN, A. 1955. "Reward Schedules and Behavior Maintained by Intracranial Self-stimulation," *Science*, **122**, 830–31.

SMITH, M., and DUFFY, M. 1955. "The Effects of Intragastric Injection of Various Substances on Subsequent Bar-Pressing," *J. Comp. Physiol. Psychol.*, **48**, 387–91.

SMITH, M. P., and CAPRETTA, P. J. 1956. "Effects of Drive Level and Experience on the Reward Value of Saccharine Solutions," *J. Comp. Physiol. Psychol.*, **49**, 553–57.

SMITH, O. A. 1956. "Stimulation of Lateral and Medial Hypothalamus and Food Intake in the Rat," *Anat. Record.*, **124**, 263–64.

SPENCE, K. W., BERGMANN, G., and LIPPITT, R. 1950. "A Study of Simple Learning under Irrelevant Motivational Reward Conditions," *J. Exper. Psychol.*, **40**, 539–51.

SPENCE, K. W., and LIPPITT, R. 1946. "An Experimental Test of the Sign Gestalt Theory of Trial-and-Error Learning," *J. Exper. Psychol.*, **36**, 491–502.

STRANGE, J. R. 1950. "Latent Learning under Conditions of High Motivation," *J. Comp. Physiol. Psychol.*, **43**, 194–97.

SUTHERLAND, N. S. 1957. "Visual Discrimination of Orientation and Shape by the Octopus," *Nature*, **179**, 11–13.

———. 1957. "Spontaneous Alternation and Stimulus Avoidance," *J. Comp. Physiol. Psychol.*, **50**, 358–62.

TEITELBAUM, P. 1955. "Sensory Control of Hypothalamic Hyperphagia," *J. Comp. Physiol. Psychol.*, **48**, 156–63.

THISTLETHWAITE, D. 1952. "Conditions of Irrelevant Incentive Learning," *J. Comp. Physiol. Psychol.*, **45**, 517–25.

THOMPSON, W. R., and HERON, W. 1954. "The Effects of Early Restriction on Activity in Dogs," *J. Comp. Physiol. Psychol.*, **47**, 77–82.

THOMPSON, W. R., and SOLOMON, L. M. 1954. "Spontaneous Pattern Discrimination in the Rat," *J. Comp. Physiol. Psychol.*, **47**, 104–7.

THOMSON, C. W., and PORTER, P. B. 1953. "Need Reduction and Primary Reinforcement: Maze Learning by Sodium-deprived Rats for a Subthreshold Saline Reward," *J. Comp. Physiol. Psychol.*, **46**, 281–87.

THORNDIKE, E. L. 1946. "Expectation," *Psychol. Rev.*, **53**, 277–81.

THORPE, W. H. 1956. *Learning and Instinct in Animals*. London: Methuen & Co.

TINBERGEN, N. 1951. *The Study of Instinct*. Oxford: Clarendon Press.

TOLMAN, E. C. 1951. *Collected Papers*. Berkeley: University of California Press.

TOLMAN, E. C., and HONZIK, C. H. 1930. " 'Insight' in Rats," *Univ. Calif. Pub. in Psychology*, **4**, 257–75.

TOWBIN, E. J. 1949. "Gastric Distention as a Factor in the Satiation of Thirst in Esophagostomized Dogs," *Amer. J. Physiol.* **159**, 533–41.

TSANG, Y. C. 1938. "Hunger Motivation in Gastrectomized Rats," *J. Comp. Psychol.*, **26**, 1–17.

VAN IERSEL, J. J. A. 1953. *An Analysis of the Parental Behaviour of the Male Three-Spined Stickleback* (gasterosteus aculeatus *L.*). Leiden: E. J. Brill.

VERNEY, E. B. 1947. "The Antidiuretic Hormone and the Factors Which Determine Its Release," *Proc. Roy. Soc. London, B*, **135**, 25–106.

WALKER, E. L. 1951. "Drive Specificity and Learning: Demonstration of a Response Tendency Acquired under a Strong Irrelevant Drive," *J. Comp. Physiol. Psychol.*, **44**, 596–603.

WOHLGEMUTH, A. 1911. "On the After-effect of Seen Movement," *Brit. J. Psychol. Monogr.*, Suppl. **1**, 1–117.

WOLF, A. V. 1958. *Thirst Physiology of the Urge To Drink and Problems of Water Lack*. Springfield, Ill.: Charles C Thomas.

YOUNG, P. T. 1948. "Appetite Palatability and Feeding Habit: A Critical Review," *Psychol. Bull.*, **45**, 289–320.

ZOTTERMAN, Y., and DIAMANT, H. 1959. "Has Water a Specific Taste?" *Nature*, **183**, 191.

Index

Kaolin, 30
Keller, 24
Kendler, 45, 73, 92, 97, 115 ff.
Kenshalo, 117
Kessen, 21, 30
kinetic theory of gases, 6–7, 10
Kivy, 49
Klüver, 136
Köhler, 15, 155–56, 159
Kohn, 21, 30

Lashley, 135, 139, 147, 156
latent learning, 84, 87, 99, 101 ff., 113 ff.
lateral nucleus of the hypothalamus, 25
learning system, uneconomical nature of, 70 ff.
Leeper, 45, 118 ff.
Lehrman, 15
Levy, 75–76
Lilly, 144–45
Link (secondary), 36 ff., 42 ff., 47, 50 ff., 54 ff., 62, 65 ff., 70, 73 ff., 78–79, 81 ff., 102 ff.
Lippitt, 92, 97, 116, 122
Long, 126
Lorenz, 15, 17, 20, 22, 27

McAllister, 116
McCann, 25
MacCorquordale, 7–8, 10, 117
McCulloch, 150
machine, 3–4, 6, 12, 13, 15, 124 ff. See also insightful learning machine
McNamara, 126
Maier, B. R. F., 86, 89, 107, 114
Marshall, 156–57
mathematical model, 6–7
mating, 18 ff., 24, 33
maze, 2, 35, 38–39, 45, 47 ff., 56, 58, 65, 69, 73, 77–78, 80, 92, 106, 110, 116 ff., 122, 124 ff., 129–30, 133
Meehl, 7–8, 10, 117
Mencher, 114
methylene blue, 33
midbrain, 65
Miller, N. E., 20–21, 25, 27, 29–30
mirror images, 135

Moltz, 76 ff.
Montgomery, K. L., 47, 49–50
Montgomery, M. F., 18
moorhen, 72
Munn, 119

nausea, 21
need, 17 ff., 56, 59–60, 62
nest-building, 52
Norton, 117
novelty, 49 ff.

octopus, 153 ff.
Olds, 65–66
orgasm, 33
Osgood, 89, 156 ff.
osmoreceptors, 24
osmotic pressure, 103
oyster catcher, 72

pain, 32, 57, 63
parrots, 70
physiological imbalance. See need
Pitts, 150
pituitary, 25
Polliard, 32
polyhydramnios, 32
Poppelreuter, 136
Porter, 32, 58, 62
potassium ions, 60
primary link, 24, 26 ff., 33 ff., 39–40, 42–43, 46, 50, 54, 56, 61–62, 56 ff., 70, 102–3
propagation of cortical waves, 143 ff.

rabbits, 52, 72
reaction potential $(S^E R)$, 76, 93–94
reactive inhibition, 47, 76
reasoning, 75, 84, 86–87, 99, 101 ff., 106 ff., 113, 127
refractory phase, 39, 47
reinforcement. See reward
reinforcement, partial, 66, 82–83, 89
retina, 137, 151, 160
reward, 45, 47, 51, 54 ff., 75, 77, 79 ff., 86, 89 ff., 93–94, 99–100, 113, 116–17, 119, 122, 171
Roby, 54, 63

saccharin, 32–33, 54–55, 63–64
saline, 58–59, 61; physiological, 57

saliva, 18
salt, 32, 59 ff. *See also* sodium deficiency
Sampliner, 29
scales, psychological, 166–67
sensory restriction, 52
Seward, 75–76
Shannon, 13
shape recognition. *See* form recognition
Sheffield, 54–55, 63
Sidman, 66
singing, 36–37, 70
Skinner box, 21, 80–81, 83
slant, 15 ff. *See also* tilt
Slater, 49 ff., 53
Smith, M., 30
Smith, M. P., 55
Smith, O. A., 25–26, 65
sodium deficiency, 58, 61. *See also* salt
sodium ions, 60
Solomon, 50
song birds, 70
special appetites, 26, 31. *See also* sodium deficiency, salt
Spence, 46, 91–92, 97, 116, 122
Stellar, 32, 60–61
Stevenson, 27
stickleback (*Gasterosteus aculeatus*), 41–42
stimulus, 3, 9, 20, 51, 55, 63, 39–40, 76–77, 79, 84 ff., 91 ff., 96–97; novel, 49 ff.
stomach, 19, 21–22, 28, 30, 46, 55, 56, 64; contractions of, 18
Strange, 117
striate cortex, 135–36
structural constructs, 9
structural explanation, 5 ff.
sucrose, 30, 64
Sutherland, 48–49, 145, 150, 153
sweet, 32, 54, 64
synaptic resistance, 12

Talbot, 156–57
Teitelbaum, 27
terminal end boutons, 12
testosterone, 33
theories, 1–14, 23–24. *See also* under specific theories
thirst, 18, 24–25, 29, 32, 45–46, 56, 62, 73, 88–89, 92, 94, 100, 108, 115 ff.
Thistlethwaite, 116
Thompson, 50, 52
Thomson, 32, 58, 62
Thorndike, 126
Thorpe, 69–70, 72
tilt, 135, 145 ff.
Tinbergen, 15, 17, 20, 22, 27, 40–41, 72
Tolman, E. C., 4–5, 106
Towbin, 29
transistors, 128
tropism, 35
Tsang, 18
Tyler, 83

urine, 32

Van Iersel, 42
ventromedial nucleus of the hypothalamus, 26–27, 64 ff.
Verney, 24
Vince, 72

Walker, 117
Wallach, 15, 155–56, 159
water intake. *See* drinking
water-salt fiber, 31
Wike, 126
Wohlgemuth, 160
Wolf, 29
Woodrow, 29
Wulff, 54

xylose, 57

Young, 32

Zotterman, 31